The Same River Twice

The Same River Twice

A MEMOIR OF DIRTBAG BACKPACKERS, BOMB SHELTERS, AND BAD TRAVEL

PAM MANDEL

Skyhorse Publishing

Skyhorse Publishing books may be purchased in bulk at special discounts for sales promotion, corporate gifts, fund-raising, or educational purposes. Special editions can also be created to specifications. For details, contact the Special Sales Department, Skyhorse Publishing, 307 West 36th Street, 11th Floor, New York, NY 10018 or info@skyhorsepublishing.com.

Skyhorse® and Skyhorse Publishing® are registered trademarks of Skyhorse Publishing, Inc.®, a Delaware corporation.

Visit our website at www.skyhorsepublishing.com.

10 9 8 7 6 5 4 3 2 1

Library of Congress Cataloging-in-Publication Data is available on file.

Cover design by Brian Peterson
Cover photo credit: Getty Images

Print ISBN: 978-1-5107-6005-9
Ebook ISBN: 978-1-5107-6100-1

Printed in the United States of America

Contents

Contents

A girl in trouble is a temporary thing.
—Romeo Void, 1984

The Same River Twice

CHAPTER ONE:
Welcome to Israel

"We have to go," the Israeli boy said, his English clear, direct. "Follow me."

I looked out the window at a black sky, at flashes of red and yellow. Was it fireworks? Why were there fireworks? I could see the outline of the mountains for a moment, then they were gone until the next flash. We pushed our chairs back and stood up, confused. The table was set with a white tablecloth. There was a golden roasted chicken, candles, the good tableware. These people were strangers. We were guests in their home for Shabbat dinner. Had we done something wrong?

"We have to go," he said again.

We followed him to the door and in the next flash, we understood. The lights weren't fireworks. They were weapons. They were bombs. We were being bombed.

"Now. Rockets."

We were out for the evening—me, my roommate Lauren, and two Israeli boys about our age. Our kibbutz volunteer program included the opportunity to make local connections. On this particular night, it meant we'd gone to Nahariya. It was the nearest town to our northern Israel kibbutz. We were having Shabbat dinner with an Israeli family to see what life was like off the kibbutz.

The boys were polite and one of them spoke good English. I was angry that I'd been assigned to go with Lauren. We had so little in common; I did not like this forced friendship. These serious boys were a good consolation prize. They drove us into town and led us to a concrete high-rise apartment where a table had been set in the living room. The apartment was small, austere. Through the boys, our hosts asked us questions about America, our families, our education. We stumbled through the kind of getting-to-know-you conversation strangers have.

Lauren was good at it; I wasn't. She liked to talk, and she wasn't embarrassed about struggling to be understood. She didn't care that she didn't speak the language. I was frustrated by my inability to communicate, by how shy I felt. I've always had a good ear for language, but it wasn't enough. I needed to relax, that's how you have real conversation, by relaxing. Not by obsessing over every single word, or worrying what people think about you. Lauren's easy manner annoyed me, and I sulked in a gray cloud of jealousy for her confidence. We ate, she talked, I sulked, and then we watched the sky light up and the boy with the good English told us we had to move. Now.

The hallway was full of people. Families spilled out of the neighboring apartments. Everyone was dressed in their Friday dinner clothes—men in clean pressed shirts, women in dresses, some with scarves tied over their hair, children with scrubbed faces. They filled the concrete stairwell as they headed to the basement. It was calm; there was no panic, no rush. There was the chatter of conversation, neighbors greeting each other on a Friday night. "Shabbat shalom," followed by a nod, a wry smile. There was this clear sense of a task to be completed, a task that had to be done right now. Footsteps echoed in the stairwell. Each time we crossed another landing, a door would

2

open, and more people would join us. We funneled downwards into the basement shelter. I squatted next to Lauren and we locked hands.

"PLO," the serious boy said. "Rockets from Lebanon."

Lauren and I looked at each other. "Are you scared?" I asked her, and she shook her head no. I was not scared either. It was hard to be scared, we had so little idea what was happening. We understood nothing of the conversation around us. Where would I have picked up the vocabulary for things like "bomb shelter," "shoulder-mounted rockets," "all-clear siren"? The lights in the sky did not look dangerous. They looked like a celebration. Nobody around us seemed scared, either. The whole situation was so matter of fact, so practiced.

When I was in grade school, we did earthquake drills and fire drills. It was a way to get out of math, if the timing was right. I remember scratchy carpet, curling up under a desk, waiting. This felt like a grade school fire drill, only it was not a drill. The bombs were real. The neighbors looked at us.

"Kibbutz volunteers. Americans," one of the boys said in Hebrew, nodding our way. I had learned the word for volunteer. I knew he was talking about us.

"Welcome to Israel," someone said in English, and everyone laughed.

CHAPTER TWO:
Anywhere But Here

"But it's such a beautiful ceremony."

I was standing in the driveway of our house, the big McMansion on a cul-de-sac, the one with the swimming pool in the back yard. Mrs. Stern had rolled down the window of her cream-colored Mercedes to ask me why I was not coming to confirmation class. I would not be going that day, not any other day. I was done.

It was Mrs. Stern's turn to drive carpool. There were four of us who rode together—her son, me, and two other kids. We were all the same age and lived just a few blocks apart, but we only saw each other on Sundays. We ignored each other the rest of the time. I was nailing the Hebrew lessons, but I hated everything else about going to class. I wasn't interested in the religious stuff. I didn't want a bat mitzvah. I didn't feel connected to anything we learned, and I wasn't making friends.

"It doesn't mean anything to me," I told Mrs. Stern, and she looked pained, like I'd insulted her personally. I didn't see the point. When I explained this to my parents, they didn't fight me.

"If it's not meaningful, you don't have to go," my parents said. I'm sure I felt relieved and then went back to whatever I was reading at the time.

I was used to spending a lot of time alone, but I was not lonely until I was a sophomore in high school. I was not lonely until the year my parents got divorced and I had to change schools. I was not lonely until I learned that boys were supposed to fit into my life somehow.

When my parents got divorced, we moved, I changed schools, and then I was lonely all the time. There are all these movies about a new girl coming to town and being taken in by a new crowd, catching the eye of some popular boy. But no one noticed the skinny new girl who didn't care about fashion, who would rather read than do anything else. There are ugly duckling myths, too—look how she is secretly very pretty!—but that was not me. I mean, maybe it could have been me, but I'd have had to care to make that transition. I'd have had to think I had something that could be revealed. I would have had to put my books down and look in the mirror to even consider changing. Or for someone to see that in me. That would have meant someone noticed me, and that simply did not happen.

It was after the second move, or maybe the third, when I barely passed advanced French. I had no excuse. I'd read *Les Misérables* in the original and, after slogging through it, could not be bothered to write a decent paper. It seems crazy that, at age fifteen, you can read a nineteenth-century classic in the original language and still fail the class, but I was up to the challenge. Language classes were easy for me, but I was not going to let that get in the way of failing. I just wanted to read; I didn't care at all about what was supposed to happen when the reading was done.

We moved, I changed schools again, I was lonely again. My new school didn't have an advanced enough French class for me to fail, so I moved on to failing Spanish and mostly being invisible in another place. I remained unsaved by the myth of the new popular girl, appreciated for her skill with languages and her apathy in the face of goals. It's just a myth anyway.

Despite my failing to deliver on the grades front, my Spanish teacher was amazed by how easy I found it to learn the language and recommended me for foreign exchange. I guess I wasn't entirely invisible. I guess she could see that my terrible classroom performance had nothing to do with my actual abilities.

"Nope," said the serious foreign exchange counselor. We were sitting in the library. The air was full of the dusty, papery smell of books. "It will be too conservative." We were sorting through destinations for my summer abroad. I had picked Switzerland; I wanted to go to the French speaking region. My second choice was Spain. "They will not let you out of the house in those places. You need to be somewhere they'll give you some room." She marked Sweden instead.

Off I went to spend the summer with a family who had a second home near the Baltic Sea. Everyone was tall and fair, and I just broke five feet. I was brown from the sun and I had a halo of blow-dried jet-black hair. One night, a leggy Swedish boy with pale skin and clear blue eyes kissed me properly for the first time on a pier that stuck out into the Baltic Sea. This handsome boy who spoke very little English thought I was worth his attention. The last thing my mom had said to me before I got on the plane to Stockholm was "Don't get pregnant!" I could not have been more virginal. The utter lack of interest any human teenage boys had shown in me made her warning comical and issued way too soon. By then, I was living with my dad and in my third high school of the year, so I did not see my mom much. Her remarks had nothing to do with me and everything to do with her possible misconception that Swedes were permissive as hell and getting it on all the time.

Maybe it was true, I don't know. But a Swedish boy kissed me. A tall boy with dark hair and such even, fair skin lay me down on the dock. He tasted like beer and cigarettes. I was stunned, dizzy, delighted. I learned a decent amount of Swedish, enough so I could order an ice cream with jam on it or buy a soda at the corner market. And then, that was all. I went back home to California—still a virgin—and back to high school and back to failing my classes as though apathy was a competitive sport.

My mom was a shadow, not really present and I didn't want to talk to her. I blamed her for my isolation, for moving us after the divorce. I didn't understand why we had to be in a new town, why we couldn't stay where we were. I didn't understand a lot of things. There were so many things no one told me about what was happening.

I overheard my parents talking about me once before they split up. We'd been going to family counseling and the therapist had said that I was, I don't remember exactly, sensitive or something. I don't remember anything shifting because of this. Maybe they figured I was old enough to understand what was happening, or maybe they didn't listen. Maybe there was no space in their lives for my troubles, given their own. They didn't treat me like a sensitive kid. They treated me like I had the skills to deal with what was happening.

I don't think they wanted to hear it from me, either. The only time my mom slapped me was after I'd said, "I don't like you very much right now." I don't remember what we were talking about—school, maybe, my grades. Or maybe it was because I was getting high all the time, coming home wasted and dizzy and checked out. She was not a violent person, but she slapped me, that one time. When you're punished for stating your feelings so clearly, it stays with you.

Not long after that fight with my mom, my friend Casey's family took me in for a semester. Casey had lived around the corner and up the hill from the house we lived in before my parents got divorced. Around the corner from that big McMansion with the swimming pool in back. Casey was freckled, soft and curvy, and pretty. When we were in junior high school, her family took me with them on their summer camping trips. I learned to water ski behind their speedboat during the day. At night, we would pull the seats in the boat into bunks while her parents slept in the camper perched on the back of their big green pickup truck.

Maybe I was living with Casey's family the year I was aggressively failing French, as though I had a point to make. I don't remember the order of things exactly. There was so much change, so much happening; it's hard to remember how everything fit together. When it all happened. But I was with Casey's family until they decided I was a bad influence.

Casey and I would slink out of the house in the middle of the night. She had a whole system figured out, a way to silently pop the screen off the downstairs window, and off we'd go. We'd smoke weed at our old elementary school and climb back into the house a few hours later. Casey knew exactly where in the house her parents could not hear her, where she could wait in the shadows to avoid being seen in passing car headlights. Sometimes the boys across the street would join us while we aimlessly wandered the neighborhood, getting high, talking nonsense, wishing we knew what to do with ourselves. But Casey's being a bad girl wasn't always after hours, sometimes we'd go on double dates, double dates her parents had signed off on. Afterwards, she'd tell me how far she'd gone while I was having

9

awkward conversations with boys who were as uncomfortable as I was in the cab of her dad's big green pickup truck.

Casey's parents knew something was up, but they didn't hear it from me. It was when Casey's report cards came that they called my parents and told them I could not stay. I was not part of the conversation about what was going to happen next. I was going to live with my dad. I guess it was his turn to deal with me. I guess I was his problem now.

I cried, hard, and considered running away the day my dad came to get me. I was in the bathroom I shared with Casey. I saw myself popping the screen of the window just like Casey did when we snuck out together, only this time, I would go alone and disappear. There was a strip of undeveloped land nearby, a shallow canyon with a little creek at the bottom, an old barn where I imagined myself hiding until I figured out what to do next. I felt completely misunderstood, blamed for trouble that I hadn't got up to. The unfairness of this, of having to hear it was my fault while staying silent to protect my friend broke me. I sat on the counter sobbing while Casey, in moment of very adult common sense, talked me down. "Where are you going to go?" she asked, and I had no answer.

In my new high school—my final high school—I had a boyfriend, Sam, who did not get me pregnant. Maybe my mom's advice was good for something. My dad and stepmom had moved to a two-story rambler on top of a hill where all the houses were big and had neat yards. My room was downstairs off the big living room where the TV was. Sam was literally from the other side of the tracks; his room was in the basement of a tumbledown old house. You had to go outside the main house, down a short flight of concrete steps, and in the back door. Sam had fuzzy pale blonde hair and dressed like a seventies rock star. He showed up for our first date wearing a leather vest and no shirt. To me, he looked like a badass, but I wish he'd worn a shirt, though my dad never said a word against him. Sam liked heavy metal, especially AC/DC, and on Halloween, he dressed like the guitar player, Angus Young, in schoolboy plaid shorts and a tie.

It was Sam's idea we should be together. He thought I was hot, and before that Swedish boy kissed me, no one had ever even mentioned my looks. It was still so new that someone would want me like this, so I went along for the ride. We hardly talked. On weekends, we went to Sam's room, got high, and went through the motions of having sex. He'd turn off all the lights except a beer sign. He'd put records on his turntable and take my clothes off. I was as interested in sex as I was in anything that wasn't reading, but I went along because it was something to do. He did not hurt me, but I did not get anything out of it, either.

I met Ian and Mackey when I transferred to my last high school. They were my first real friends since my family started moving around, since I started getting shifted like so much furniture. Ian, Mackey, and I went to movies and the mall and acted like adults by going to eat in chain restaurants. Mackey had a car, a Mustang convertible, white with a red interior. We cruised the El Camino, the main drag lined with strip malls and supermarkets and two-story motels. We played the radio, and drove around aimlessly, talking about school and boys and music and how we had no idea what we were going to do once we'd graduated.

Ian was tall and thin and had perfect feathered hair. He was always dressed in corduroy pants and striped polo shirts, and when the weather was warm, he swapped the pants for corduroy shorts. He was unbreakably cheerful, and his smile went all the way into his blue-gray eyes. Ian was gay and had not told anyone. It's possible he didn't know at the time, either. People called him gay as an insult, but it wasn't until we were well out of high school, much, much later, that he was all, "Yeah, I am totally gay."

Mackey was just different, like a sassy fifties waitress stuck in this seventeen-year-old red-headed girl. She was so solidly herself and didn't apologize to anyone for it. Her parents seemed old to me, but they adored Mackey and spoiled her. They gave her that Mustang for her sixteenth birthday, and she had tons of freedom, but she didn't act spoiled at all. She was never jealous of things she didn't have, and she didn't act like she deserved anything, ever. Funny and sweary and impatient with people who were mean, Mackey was a whirlwind of fun and common sense. She was the first person I knew with a tattoo and she drove like she was trying to outrace the police after a bank robbery. She was terrible at schoolwork, but no way could you say she wasn't smart. She didn't care about book learning, that's all. It was like she was biding her time until she could be twenty-one or thirty or older, even, and live a grown-up life on her own.

And there was me, with my books and my Spanish and my French and my third high school. We did not fit anywhere, so we hung out together.

On the weekends, we'd go to the drive-ins in Mackey's car, put the top down, and forget about the movie. Ian would sprawl across the narrow back seat, his feet up on the edge of the car, and Mackey and I would tilt the front seats back. We'd smoke a joint and stare at the stars, talking about nothing until the credits rolled.

Mackey's dad was a DeLorean-driving mechanic. There was always some half-built car in the driveway at their house, a tiny two-bedroom place full of kitschy knickknacks. I rarely went to Ian's house, though it seems like he was always in my kitchen after school. They were the only thing I liked about my senior year—Ian's consistent smile and Mackey's profanity laced common sense. Everything else had no color. I didn't care about any of it. I didn't even care about Sam, my boyfriend, not really. I liked having a boyfriend. It made me feel more normal, like the kind of person who could have a boyfriend. But Sam and I weren't friends. When we weren't getting high and making out or pretending to go to the movies but instead having unsatisfying sex in his basement room, we didn't have much to talk about. Sam was probably going to be a plumber, like his dad. I liked books about art history; I liked reading about Picasso and Da Vinci. I liked words and foreign languages. Sam and I didn't have much in common besides our high school boredom.

I wanted to drop out and go directly to the community college, but my dad was insistent about my getting a high school diploma. Instead of dropping out, I simply stopped going to classes that bored me. My Spanish teacher apologized when I asked him about my mediocre grade. I had aced all the tests. "I can't give you an A because you don't come to class," he said. "I'm sorry."

During school hours, I'd been going for long walks and smoking weed with my outcast group of non-friends, Sam's friends, really. While Ian and Mackey went to class, I'd leave campus with this handful of bored kids and walk up the steep hill behind the school. There were a lot of construction sites up there; we'd wander the skeletons of future oversized houses, not talking to each other, passing a sticky joint between us, laughing at the perfect California sky when the high kicked in. I should have been in algebra or English or history. I preferred the feeling of sun-warmed concrete while I lay on my back watching clouds drift by overhead.

My group of outsiders stayed in our corner on campus and smoked cigarettes. Sometimes we went to each other's houses after school if no parents were home. We smoked pot in nice fenced yards, rummaging in kitchen cabinets for Cheez-its crackers, polishing off Haagen Dazs ice cream from the freezer. Sometimes we figured out how to get to concerts and saw anthem rock bands; maybe someone's big sister drove us home late at night.

One of the girls, her dad traveled a lot and he left her home alone. We'd all would spend the night at her house. We'd stay up late snorting cocaine off the glass-topped coffee table, playing Boston and Journey and Styx until we crashed, early in the morning. Ian's brother had a hookup. We'd wait in someone's car while Ian stood in the garage handing our money to his brother's dealer. We blew our allowances on drugs and vinyl records and concert tickets.

This is who I was, what I was like when I stepped out into the world. A bookish suburban California kid who smoked a fair bit of weed, dabbled in some harder drugs, skipped a lot of school. Now, they'd probably say I was depressed and self-medicating; they'd send me off to therapy. But it was the late seventies and it seemed like we were supposed to know what we were doing at fifteen. It was okay to leave us to our own devices, day after day. We were expected to figure out how to be adults on our own.

During my last year in high school, my dad was in trouble. Someone had delivered something for him, a big envelope. I'd left it in the kitchen and told him later that day.

"Did you sign for it?" he asked.

"I don't remember if he asked me to. I don't think he asked me to. Maybe I did. I don't know."

"Didn't I tell you never to sign for anything? Did I not tell you that? Those guys are process servers. Do. Not. Sign. Anything. Ever." His voice kept getting louder. I did not know what I'd done wrong. The guy rang the bell and handed me an envelope. He was just a delivery guy as far as I knew.

"What's a process server?"

A process server, my dad explained, was the guy who brought the papers that required you to show up in court. If you made it hard to be served by not accepting the papers, or just avoiding these guys all together, you didn't have to go to court. You weren't responsible for charges you didn't know anything about.

My dad ran an electronics export business out of the house. Our basement was full of weird devices, including a telex machine that rattled in the middle of the night when orders came in from Hong Kong. We had two phone lines, one where we got calls, the other sitting in the cradle of the telex machine, ready to receive messages from buyers. There were big cardboard boxes and Styrofoam insets and tape guns and always the clacking noise of the telex printer. My dad was a reseller, and sometimes he shipped machines, ones with knobs and numerical displays and dials, to foreign countries. That's why I wasn't supposed to take papers from anyone. The United States federal government wanted to talk to my dad about his business. He very much did not want to talk to them.

My dad and stepmom were always pretending to have more money than they really did. I could hear them talking about their troubles when they did not know I was listening. Mostly it was about money, I didn't really understand the other stuff they would talk about. I just knew our fancy neighborhood house on the hill was going up for sale and we were going to move again. I was afraid it would happen before I finished high school and then what? Another school? Another restart?

My last year of high school was about surviving long enough to get the piece of paper that let me do other things. I got called into the school counselor once. Everything in the office was washed out, including the counselor, a stocky woman in a beige suite. I sat on a metal classroom chair next to her institutional green desk.

"You have to get these grades up or you're not going to college," she told me.

"Yeah, community college," I said. "Isn't that what community college is for?"

It was so boring to be that girl who fell into bad company, the smart girl who lost interest in school when her home life unraveled. Where had this supposedly helpful advisory adult been over the last year? I was supposed to be planning for college? How? Who was going to pay for it? It seemed impossible, like going to the moon. This post-high school future was a foggy wasteland.

A random beige adult in a random office I visited one time in my last year in high school was not going to inspire me to buckle down and work harder. It was too late, anyway. Graduation wasn't that far away. I had more than three years of unnoticed, unchecked apathy behind me; I could not go back and change it.

I was seventeen the year I graduated high school. I just wanted to be somewhere else.

"You're going to Israel. For the summer. With a youth group."
If I had not dropped out of confirmation, I probably would have known this was a thing. High school graduates, first-year college students, they joined tour groups and went to the so-called Promised Land to learn about their heritage. They sang songs and did farm work and met actual Israelis. They met the people they would have become if their grandparents had gone to Israel after World War II instead of going to America after World War I, like mine did.

"It's your graduation present," my dad said.

"Thank you?" I said. "Okay?"

Graduation was looming and I had completed exactly zero college applications. I didn't have the grades or the extracurricular activities to get into university. I was saving what pocket money I did not spend on bus fare and weed with the idea that after high school, I would get a job, maybe get my own place. But I didn't understand how that would work. At seventeen, I was underage. No one was going to rent to me. I would have to get a roommate who was old enough. Once I figured that out, what would be next?

Shipping off to another foreign country was a good an option as any.

My parents were the children of first-generation Jewish immigrants. Their grandparents had left Central Europe to get away from Fiddler on the Roof-style Cossacks, the kind that kept moving Jewish villages around before burning them to the ground. Cue "Anatevka," that song where the villagers talk about what a lousy place their town is but they're still really sad to leave it. That was my great grandparents.

My dad had a few stories about family history, but I don't know how true they were. Because I wasn't close to my grandparents—geographically or otherwise—I never asked them. My dad said he had a grandfather, or maybe a great uncle, or maybe he was on my mother's side, I don't remember. Anyway, he was a total commie and, if you believe my dad, a thief, too. He worked as a plumber, or for a plumbing supply company, and would come home with cast-iron plumbing tools. He'd schlep these heavy stolen objects—a pipe threader, a giant monkey wrench—up the stairs into their tenement apartment in the Bronx. This relative may or may not have been the same character that considered himself an artist and apparently was always quitting his job to stay home and paint. But he was not very good, so it didn't work out as a career choice. My dad also said someone in his family was the right-hand man to a famous union organizer and that my uncle—his brother, who was skinny and brown—used to get beat up by white kids because he was dark. He'd get all kinds of slurs thrown at him and he'd shout, "But I'm not Mexican, I'm Jewish!" while trying to fend off the blows. I want all these stories to be true, but my dad was never a reliable source.

In our house, we observed some of the holidays—Hanukkah, Passover, Yom Kippur, and the Jewish New Year—but it pretty much collapsed to Passover as time went by. My dad wore a big gold star and he looked Jewish. There was no getting around his big nose, his dark receding hair. He didn't worry so much about the specifics of religious practice, but Jewish culture—Jewish identity—was important to him. Before I quit confirmation lessons, he had a fight with our temple. The other Hebrew school parents were mad because my dad had said that Jews were, well, better. He really bought into the whole Chosen People thing. "It's in THE TORAH," he'd shout, "It SAYS we're the Chosen People. Of course we're better!" Our reform temple told him he couldn't say that Jews were better, and he was mad about that. It was probably just as well I didn't want to go anymore, because he wasn't super welcome.

Dad was an anti-racist activist too. My parents got into all kinds of trouble with the neighborhood when my dad ran for the school board. He wanted school integration in our rich mostly white neighborhood while many of our rich, mostly white neighbors did not want that at all. Years later, decades later, my mom told me they used to get hate mail and threatening phone calls because of my dad's activism.

The little I knew about Israel came from the story of Passover and watching Charlton Heston's *The Ten Commandments* when it aired on television around Easter time. I knew Israel was a sort of Jewish homeland, though I did not know why it existed. I imagined it to be a desert oasis reached by crossing the Red Sea on foot. Could that be right? And I knew one day we were all—we, I mean the entire Jewish people—meant to live there like it was an endless Jewish summer camp. There would be singing. By some miracle of agriculture, this dry, sand-swept wasteland would produce a lot of fruits and vegetables. The trip my dad signed me up for was supposed to teach me about the homeland, about my culture and history. My time would be

19

spent working on a kibbutz, whatever that was, and taking field trips to see the country.

I didn't bother to learn anything about where I was going. No one gave me a guidebook. I didn't ask for one. I didn't go to the library; I didn't do any homework at all. I went along for the ride because I had no better ideas. I figured a trip to Israel would be a rerun of my time as an exchange student in Sweden only with Jewish kids and better weather. I packed my Walkman, a stack of mix tapes, and boarded a plane from San Francisco to New York.

I found my tour group when I changed planes in at JFK Airport. The organization had sent us pale blue T-shirts with white lettering; the other kids were hard to miss. There were twelve of us, evenly split between boys and girls, and a sort of camp counselor, Diane, barely older than the rest of the group. She might have been twenty-one. She cannot have been a day older.

Diane was blonde and fit and looked like a surfer. Not at all like the dark-haired Jewish kids I had met at Hebrew school. Diane counted heads and assigned us to our rooms, but she wasn't there to babysit or teach. If no one was missing from the bus after a field trip, that was good enough for her. She occasionally rummaged something out of a first-aid kit for sunburn or a headache or a bad belly. She helped us understand what we'd signed up for, but she didn't tell us what to do. She was bossy only when someone inconvenienced her or acted bratty or stubborn, but that wasn't her usual manner. Mostly she treated us like younger friends. It was not her job to keep us from drinking beer or smoking or ending up in each other's beds. She just needed us to be where we were supposed to be when we were supposed to be there. She spoke fluent Hebrew, took no shit from any-one, and expected us all to solve our own problems.

At seventeen, I was the youngest in my group, but I was not the most sheltered by a long shot. Lauren was cute and extroverted and got a lot of attention from the boys. I had never known a so-called JAP—Jewish American Princess—before. JAP is a stereotype of a particular type of spoiled Jewish girl, and Lauren was the textbook definition. She had shiny jewelry and perfect hair and she put on makeup before we went to work in the fields. I owned makeup, a little, but I could not be bothered with it, certainly not enough to take it with me on this trip. Everything in Lauren's wardrobe had a label on it. Her fashion sense came right from the women's magazines that came to my stepmom in the weekly mail. Most of the time, I was dressed in a pair of cutoffs and a t-shirt, while Lauren wore shirts with collars and blow-dried her hair before leaving our room. For the first week or so, I judged Lauren silently every time I was in her com-pany. Then we ended up in that bomb shelter together. We never really became friends but after what we'd been through, it was hard to look at her without going right back to the shelter, our hands locked while we waited for the all clear siren to blow. After that, I stopped being so bitchy towards her. She was kind and friendly and that's how I tried to see her.

The kibbutz was in northern Israel. It was sort of what I imagined a college campus would look like. There was a broad driveway through a main gate, flanked on both sides by uniformed soldiers. Once we were inside the gate any feeling of military dropped away. Our housing was closest to the gate, a cluster of one-story buildings with dorm style rooms, each room housing four workers. There was a large cafeteria with a high ceiling and big windows along one side; that's where we'd get our meals three times a day. Neat green lawns flanked the cafeteria. There was a swimming pool and covered walk-ways between the buildings for shade. The kibbutz teenagers and young adults lived in housing similar to—but much nicer than—ours. Families with smaller kids and married couples lived in stuccoed duplexes and fourplexes. There was a dairy barn full of fat, docile cows, and the air was sharp with the smell of cow poop. Just adjacent to the dairy, there was a stable with a few horses for recreational rid-ing. The property was surrounded by acres of crops, tough but abun-dant apple trees and rows and rows of cotton. I don't think it ever rained; the skies were blue and clear all day every day. At night the sky was full of stars.

Our day-to-day work as volunteer farm hands was physical but not particularly challenging. We needed endurance but not a lot of strength. We dressed while it was still dark and headed to the cafete-ria where we shuffled around drinking instant coffee and eating dry biscuits, blinking in the bright artificial light. We'd join a work crew and tumble into the back of a van for transport to the site we'd be working that day. My group had been assigned to the cotton fields. It seemed ironic that we'd come all this way to do a job that was such a cornerstone of American history. I knew we had it easy, though. I wasn't so naïve to think that the work we were doing was anything like working in the fields in Mississippi or Alabama. We had chosen to be here. We were treated well.

The soil was soft and well-tilled. The weeds weren't hard to pull out of the ground, but the work had to be done by hand to protect the plants. The first time I saw an actual cotton pod, I pulled it apart and stabbed my fingers on the spiky seeds hidden in the floss. We walked for miles every day, up and down the long rows, coaxing weeds from the soil without disturbing the plants. We'd drop the uprooted weeds on to the bare dirt between the rows where they'd die in the bright sunshine. While we walked, miles and miles over the course of our shifts, we talked about home and what we would study in college when we got there. We talked about what kind of music we liked and what books we were reading and when we were out of words, we walked in silence. We'd stop for a real breakfast later in the morning, sometimes in a shed on the edge of the fields; sometimes back in the cafeteria, depending on how far we were from the center of the kibbutz. After breakfast, we'd work until the sun was high in the sky and it was too hot to continue. We put in about six hours, starting before sunrise and working until lunch, and then we were done for the day.

We were free in the afternoons. We'd sleep off the early morning or sit in the shade drinking beer we'd bought from the commissary. No one cared that I was too young to be drinking beer, and the beer was just soda weight anyway. We smoked cigarettes and spit sunflower shells everywhere, a habit we'd picked up from the Israeli soldiers who were our neighbors. We traded cassette tapes with anyone who had music to share and went to the pool. We argued about the world because all of a sudden, we were in it and had ideas we'd never had before. I read the *Jerusalem Post* almost every day because it was in English and it was something to read. I was always hungry for something to read.

I hadn't forgotten what little language I'd learned in Hebrew school. I picked up vocabulary the way a bird picks up stray bits of string and shiny wrappers for a nest. The Israelis I met wanted to talk to me, wanted to teach me, wanted me for one of them. I found the attention flattering, and I liked the way my days unfolded. I liked getting up before dawn and watching the sky brighten. I liked sharing my days with the other volunteers. I even liked walking the fields for hours, a sort of mediation in motion. The work was made of heat and miles and dirt, but it was satisfying. I had three meals day and hot showers and a comfortable bed. Nearly every evening with my new friends felt like a party. The life was easy, appealing, and I felt included. The experience was getting under my skin; I was becoming sold on the idea that this hot dry place was supposed to be my home.

When I was fourteen or so, a middle school friend told me her dad said she should be careful about "spending too much time with those people." I knew we were different, but this was the first time I learned being Jewish made me different in what could be seen as a bad way. My friend ended up pregnant by a homeless guy who hung out in a local park near our high school. It sounds made up, but it's true. He was in his thirties; she was barely sixteen. They would have sex in the park bathroom. Her parents made her have the baby and give it up for adoption. I don't remember if the guy went to jail for rape. My friend said she loved him. She told me this when I was talking to her on the phone from wherever it was they'd sent her. She was bored all the time: being pregnant was boring, she said, and she spent most of her time reading magazines and sleeping. I didn't hear from her much after the baby was born and we lost touch after I moved away again. I missed her but I could never think of her without remembering what her dad had said. "Don't spend too much time with those people."

In Israel, nearly everyone I encountered was Jewish, and that was new—not having to explain what it meant to be Jewish, not having that outsider feeling, not being "those people." I was with Jewish kids who understood we had this thing in common, in a country full of people where we also had this thing in common. I started to forget what it felt like to be lonely, to be different. The California suburbs and all that moving around, the three different high schools and the weirdly unsettling situation back home gradually faded into the background.

CHAPTER FOUR:
Israeli Exit Strategy

Here's what I knew about politics when I got to Israel: Not much. Here's what I learned not long after I arrived. Ronald Reagan was the American president and that was bad. I mean, I knew he was president, but I don't think I knew this was a good or bad thing, not really. Margaret Thatcher was the Prime Minister of Great Britain and that was also bad. Helmut Schmidt was the chancellor of Germany and, you guessed it: bad. The US was in a nuclear arms race with Russia and that was really, really bad.

I had some basic ideas about the cold war because we had nuclear attack drills in grade school when I was still very young. The Russians had weapons that could obliterate us. To protect ourselves, we were to duck under our desks, curled up with our hands protecting the backs of our necks. There was a cartoon about this featuring a turtle and a song, "Duck and Cover." This posture might save us from the initial blast, but afterwards, there would be radiation. It would cause us to glow in the dark, to be eaten alive from the inside out, to become actual zombies. To avoid this, we were meant to hide out underground, in shelters kitted with everything we would need until the radiation went away. We were also supposed to be afraid of Russian submarines off the coast of California. They could be out there, up to no good.

Once, in high school, I went on a double date with Mackey. She'd set me up with a cute blonde surfer boy. While Mackey and her guy were making out on the beach, I sat in the back seat of Mackey's car listening to this guy talk about how he was never getting married, never having kids, because we were all going to die in a nuclear blast, so what was the point. I did not go out with him again.

According to my kibbutz volunteer friends, some of them college students who knew a lot more about politics than I did, Russia was changing, or trying to change. America was still deep in a one-sided cold war mentality. To hear it from my friends, the American government was bad. Reagan had walked away from a chance to make peace with our enemies. He had some crazy idea about weapons in space that was more important.

Meanwhile, in Europe, unemployment was high and young adults were shit out of luck, no matter how educated they were. Young Europeans came to Israel to work for a bed, three meals a day, and a small stipend that paid for beer. These Europeans, mostly German and British, but some from other countries, had a completely different agenda than the kids I'd arrived with. They weren't seeking a tie to their homeland. They weren't trying to understand their cultural identity. They weren't spending an adventurous summer abroad. They were trying to survive an economy that had no place for them. In Israel, they found everything they needed to wait out the bad times back home. Beer and cigarettes were cheap, and the kibbutz offered medical care—they'd even send you to a dentist in town if you needed it. Unemployed twenty-somethings, fleeing crippling depression—nothing to do, no work, no money—used the kibbutz volunteer program like a waiting room. Israel was a place to hang out until the tide rose in their home countries.

The Germans and the Brits looked down on the Jewish American volunteers. They acted like we were rich kids, and maybe compared to them we were. They figured our parents had spent good money to send us on these working vacations. We were happy to be away from home. They were not. They were a little bit older than we were, at the end of their luck and their money. We were all just starting out on our adult lives. The kids I was with were so optimistic about what was going to happen next. We'd go home and start college or live with our parents until we got jobs. The Europeans didn't have these options. They didn't know when they could go home again, or what they would find when they got there.

Once I saw a bird hit a window. It got completely knocked out and slid down the glass until it hit the ground. It sat there, stunned to find its flight interrupted. I think they were like that, interrupted, and angry. They mocked us just within earshot and we pretended not to understand them. They worked longer hours than we did, they drank harder and smoked more than we did, they stayed up later. We all shared the same housing and we worked together, but we were not like them. We were not going to be friends, not if they could help it.

The kibbutz was supposed to be founded on egalitarian values, but there was a pecking order. It was the kibbutz residents, those families first, of course. Then the young Jewish volunteers—that was us. Maybe we'd build the next generation of kibbutz families if things played out the way they were supposed to. Right on our heels, or maybe next to us, were the Israeli soldiers assigned to the kibbutz for security. Next rung down on the ladder? Paid workers, people who lived in town and came to do seasonal jobs. Sometimes they were Arabs—Israeli Arabs who spoke Hebrew and were longtime residents of the country. They might come from families who lived there even before Israel was established. And last, the Germans, the British, with the longest hours, the lowest pay, and the least likelihood of finding a connection to the place.

In the summer of 1981—not long before I'd arrived on the kibbutz—the Israeli army bombed Lebanon. It was in response to rockets coming over the border into Israel. The same rockets that lit up the sky that night I went to dinner in town with my roommate Lauren. These programs that bring Jewish kids in from overseas to imprint on the homeland don't tell you that there were already people here when the Jewish state was founded. A whole lot of people with a long history of their own. You learn about the Arab-Israeli War of 1948 and how a bunch of scrappy Holocaust survivors claimed the land and built their nation here. How they fought with the surrounding Arab countries to solidify that claim. But anything that's not Israeli-centric gets skimmed over with almost no context. I didn't know that my summer program that took place in a country that had been in a near endless war with the people who had been pushed out when the first Israelis occupied this strip of land on the Mediterranean. I didn't know that the lights in the sky were the rebellious act of a displaced people who'd been angry with Israel for more than thirty years.

When the bombs started falling, we slept in bomb shelters at night. My group was assigned to bunk with the kibbutz teenagers. Under thick layers of cool concrete, we traded our band t-shirts and college sweatshirts for their blue work shirts. We watched movies and sprawled like puppies in the triple high bunks. The Germans and Brits were in the shelter near our bunk houses, doing we didn't know what. It would not have occurred to us to go find out. We were having sleepover parties with our de facto little brothers and sisters, our future cousins.

I was fascinated by the Germans. I secretly kind of wanted to be one of them. They had the same out-of-sync vibe coming off them that I felt in high school. The Jewish kids I was with, they were awesome. I liked them, and for the first time I was with people I could be easy friends with. They liked me too. But the Germans—they seemed, I don't know, sharper, like they had spikes on them. They were tough. The kibbutz kids felt like family, and my youth group, they were suburban kids like me. But the Germans and the Brits, they were punk. Skinny and rough and sunburned, always wearing torn t-shirts. I wanted to be punk too. I wanted to be punk even after one of the Germans crawled into my bed in the middle of the night, uninvited.

It was just another night when it happened. I heard the door open and saw the light from the porch slice across the floor. Then he was in my bed, crushing me. I was dull with sleep, but as soon I realized what was happening, I tried to scream. He put one hand over my mouth and gently slapped my face. "I'm not going to hurt you," he said. "Quiet, little one." When he spoke, I recognized the voice: Hannes.

We never locked our doors. Why would we? We knew everyone and the place was—what's the expression? *Safe as houses*. Even though we'd been shelled, even though we sometimes slept in shelters, I always felt safe. It was a ridiculous place to be a thief. Everyone knew everyone else, and the constant security meant that there was no one around who wasn't supposed to be there. No one around who didn't have a reason to be there.

Hannes smelled like beer and cigarettes. I could hear my voice in my ears, leaking out from under his hand into the dark room. "Get off me," I cried, "Go away." It must have been louder than it seemed inside my head. In the opposite corner of the room, Kelly, one of my roommates, sat up in bed and said, "Hey, are you okay?" Maybe she thought I was having a nightmare. I feel like I could see her sit up, but that cannot have been possible because I was pinned under Hannes. He said something in German and rolled off me. Kelly flipped on her bedside light. "What's going on?" she said, and Hannes staggered from the room. Kelly rushed over. I sat up and wrapped myself in my blanket.

I had three roommates: Lauren, Kelly, and Jules. Kelly was a California girl like our group leader, blonde and sunshiny and independent—we did not spend a lot of time together. Jules was bookish, like me, and fair with dark hair. We weren't close, but she was kind to me because I helped her when she came down with sunstroke. I was the one who had sent for help when she woke up feverish and crying with pain in the middle of the night. I sat with her, laying cold, wet towels on her bright red skin until the doctor came.

"I'm fine," I said. "He just . . . it was Hannes. I think he was drunk."

Kelly had turned the overhead light on. Lauren and Jules were awake now too. We looked at each other in the too bright light.

"Are you sure you're okay?" said Kelly.

"I really am. Honest. He scared me, but he did not hurt me." Lauren and Kelly were sitting on either side of me. "It was Hannes," I said again. "He must have been drunk."

Jules was sitting up, too, directly across from me, blinking in the bright light. "We have to tell someone," she said. She got up and locked the door.

"I'm fine. Really. We have to work in the morning and I'm fine. Let's talk about it tomorrow. Go to sleep. The door is locked, right?"

The next day, Sophia, another volunteer, quizzed me mercilessly.

"Are you sure you weren't inviting it?" she asked.

"Sophia, no. Of course not."

Sophia was an outspoken feminist, a lesbian from Santa Cruz. She was the first person close to my age I'd ever met who defined herself as a feminist. Before I met her, my idea of feminism was something our moms did so girls could play sports and grow up to have jobs that weren't just secretarial. I understood that feminism was important, but it was also the punch line to a joke. Helen Reddy's I Am Woman topping the charts in 1972. Tennis player Billie Jean King beating Bobby Riggs at a show match in 1973. But it never occurred to me that there were things I could not do as a girl.

I also knew I wasn't good at being a girl in the way I was supposed to in order to get along in the world. My mom was good at these things that women were supposed to do. She was stylish, she could sew, and she was pretty. My stepmom was good at it, and she was pretty too. She spent money on the kinds of things that helped women package themselves as attractive to men, fashion, makeup, jewelry, the right shoes. I was bad at all of it, at doing my hair and putting the right outfit together and saying things that got you attention from boys.

In the late 70s, there was a TV ad for perfume that mashed these things up, the idea of feminism and being pretty, sexy. Everyone knew the words. "I can bring home the bacon, fry it up in a pan, and never ever let you forget you're a man." That was what I understood feminism was at the time—you could do your own thing, but at the end of the day, it was how your power made a man feel. I didn't know how to do any of it, not how to be cool in the world, and certainly not how make a man *feel* things.

For my new friend Sophia, it was different. It was about owning your place in the world, about demanding to be treated fairly.

Feminism was about women, not where women fit into men's lives. Sophia was chubby and cute, her dark hair cut in a short bob. She was strong and wore t-shirts with the sleeves cut off so you could see the hair in her unshaved armpits.

"What about those shorts you wear?" she said. "They're pretty short."

"What's that got to do with anything?"

"That's the right answer."

I don't know who told our group leader about what had happened, but everyone was looking at me sideways when we came back from the fields that day. Hannes glared at me like I was the one who'd been out of bounds.

"You tattled," he spat at me from the door of his room. He was angry with me, but I had done nothing wrong. I turned hot with embarrassment under his angry gaze. Hannes had flirted at me—not with me, exactly, but at me, throwing words in my direction in a way that made me uncomfortable. He flirted with me like a joke, for show. "Ha ha, look how I make this young American girl blush." He told anyone who would listen that he'd been trying to find a place to hide so he could skip out on work the next day. If he stayed in his own room, someone would fetch him for his shift; chase him out of bed to the fields. He had been drunk; I was right. But I was confused by how guilty I felt. How was any of this my fault? None of the Germans would look me in the eye. A few days later, Hannes was gone.

"Respect yourself," Sophia told me. She was sitting in the shadow of the bomb shelter entry, the shelter where the Germans went during air raid drills. It was early evening; I was taking photos of the concrete silo with the camera I'd received as a graduation present. I clicked the shutter when I was happy with the way the sharp shadows lined up with the angles of the shelter.

"Don't I?"

She shook her head at me. "Let's go get dinner," she said.

Israeli soldiers were assigned to the kibbutz as part of their army service. They sat in the box at the front gate or circled the grounds at night as security. They carried machine guns and dressed in olive green. During the air raid drills, they disappeared. We did not know where they went, and they didn't tell us. They shouldered their guns and walked off, unhurried.

Between their shifts, the Israeli boys sat on the porch in front of their rooms and looked at us like they were hungry and we were food. The girls all swooned. These boys were no more than nineteen or twenty years old, and they were very fit. They had big soft eyes and a sort of smudgy look about them like they'd just got out of bed no matter what time of day it was. They looked at us, at all the American girls, like they were going to go lie down, and their roommates were out for at least four hours and they knew we wanted to go lie down with them. Like they knew what we wanted, even if we didn't. The door was unlocked; it was just a matter of time before we kicked off our shoes and went inside.

Unlike Hannes, with the mean streak under his teasing, the Israelis were completely without irony. They would look right at you, an invitation. They were biding their time until you showed up in their bed. Not only did they know you'd be there eventually, they knew you would be grateful once you had. Their confidence was shocking, intoxicating, shameless.

No one had looked at me that way before, ever. Not the Swedish boy when I was an exchange student, not my high school boyfriend, no one. It was almost physical, though they never put their hands on me in an inappropriate way. It made me feel like I had something hidden that only these Israeli guys could see. The way they looked at me made me feel like I had dared them to find it.

They had names we knew, David and Micah and Joshua, but they taught the girls how to say them with Israeli accents, Dah-veed and Mee-kah and Yosh-oo-ah. Slowly. They'd correct us and stare at our American mouths while we strung out the vowels. They tried to teach us to make them rounder than our flat American accents allowed. In the cafeteria where we had all our meals, they'd hurl themselves into chairs across from us and talk at us in Hebrew. Confounded that we could not understand them, they'd switch to English as though we were simple. But they always started in Hebrew, like they expected us to understand them overnight. They'd be sitting outside smoking, spitting sunflower shells when we wandered back from work, covered with dust and sweat. One of them would raise a chin; another would lift one corner of his mouth in a half-smile, and that was enough. Making eye contact with one of these young soldiers was, no question, the sexiest thing I had ever experienced.

The things the Israeli boys said were completely out of sync with their eyes. They wanted to invite me home—to eat baba ghanoush, to meet their mothers. They meant it. I did not understand that yes, they absolutely wanted to fuck me, very much so. But more than that, they wanted to get married. And none of it had anything to do with me.

Part of their endless hunger was the very real possibility that their lives could end tomorrow. Today they were assigned to patrol the perimeter of the kibbutz at night, but their next assignment could see them on border with Lebanon where they might die in an attack, the same attacks we sought shelter from at night. They might be stationed in the West Bank to work a checkpoint where they'd endure the angry

34

taunting and rock throwing from Palestinians who did not want them there. Any day could be the day they were mobilized never to return. They grabbed what life they could when they had the chance.

But it was not just an end-of-the-world free-for-all—let's fuck today because tomorrow we might be dead. They were strategists, too. The Michas and the Joshuas and the Davids wanted out. They wanted my passport; they wanted the passport from any American girl in their crosshairs. Their aggressive flirting, the way they looked at me, at all the American girls, the thing I was hiding from them was American citizenship. They dreamed of snagging an American wife, of getting beyond Israel's narrow borders and into the endless possibilities of an imaginary bright American future. They wanted out of this land of endless wars. The American dream was all too real for them, they believed every shred of the myth and they wanted it for themselves.

Not only was I Jewish, but I came from the best place, California, so I was a golden ticket. Just like the Germans, the Israelis assumed I was rich because my father had sent me to this faraway place. I was playing at kibbutz, playing at Israeli with my clunky but increasingly functional Hebrew. It was cute and when it was over, I would return to the real Promised Land of San Mateo, California. Maybe I could take one of them with me.

The game of snagging an American girl was a near daily ritual with the soldiers. My volunteer group would walk past their bunk house every afternoon after lunch. The soldiers would be out front in the shade of the overhang.

"Come sit with me," one of them would coax. There was nowhere I had to be, and they were so good looking. I almost always said yes. "Have a cigarette. Tell me about California. You live at the beach, yes?"

"No. I live in the suburbs. A house in a neighborhood."

"With a swimming pool, yes? What kind of car does your father drive? You have a boyfriend? How many children will you have when you get married? Repeat after me . . ." They'd say something profane. "Say it first, then I'll tell you what it means."

These conversations felt like a job interview where there were no wrong answers. It didn't matter what I answered, I already had the job. While we talked, they would lean in to take a lock of hair between their fingers, to tap my knee, to wrap a warm hand around my arm. "The work is making you strong," and there would be that look. "You have hair like a Sabra," they would say. "You could be Israeli. I could be American, yes? If we got married, I could be American, right?

I'd laugh. "Yes, I suppose you could," I'd say.

"What kind of job does your father have? Did you say? I can work for him, my English is very good."

And they'd lean in more, like my nationality was something they could acquire if they just got close enough to me.

The fact that I was American was enough to make them want to swallow me whole.

CHAPTER FIVE:
American Girls, Israeli Boys

Dave was from San Diego, but he spoke English like it was a foreign language. He had a smooth, muscled chest and peeled off his shirt at every possible opportunity. I guess he was hot, but the way he talked, no one could quite figure him out. We would look at him, his surfer's body, but no one wanted to hook up with him because talking to him was so weird.

Dave wanted me. He said so. He was always on my heels. He told me that he did not know Jewish girls could be pretty until he met me. He was always putting himself in the way so I could not do anything without interacting with him.

I could not decide if he was making fun of me or was just a bit dense. Every other girl in our group was more put together than I was; it made no sense that he should set his sights on me. I told him to stop mocking me. He acted like I was teasing and did not leave me alone. He was always nearby, trying to be helpful. Always trying to win me over by loading my plate in the cafeteria, offering to help me down out of the tractor trailer, saving me a seat next to him on the bus, but I was annoyed by his attentions.

When you've been an ugly duckling you never stop seeing the ugly in the mirror. Back when I was in high school, guys like Dave wouldn't look up if I called them by name. I didn't think I had changed much in the weeks I'd been in Israel. Was it because everyone wore glasses to keep the sun out of their eyes, so mine weren't the default mark of uncool anymore? I had turned brown from the sun, and there were muscles under my skin from the field work. But inside, I was still a pile of books with dog-eared pages. I looked at the other girls with their makeup, their fitted shirts, their completeness. Even in the fields they looked like they dressed to be seen. I believed that's what boys wanted, not the baggy sweatshirts I wore to hide my bony chest, not my flya-way hair. When I listened to boys talk about girls, it was almost always about what they looked like. I did not look anything like what they were talking about.

And there was Evan. I wished Evan had been my high school boyfriend. He was going to start classes at UC Berkeley after the summer was over. He was smart and, like me, a reader. He was tall and skinny and wore corduroy shorts and University of California at Berkeley t-shirts and we shared the newspaper often. He was nerdy, but kind of cool, and while he joked with the boys when they checked out the girls, he seemed embarrassed about it. I liked him a lot—really liked him—and one night, I followed him down to the place where the lights from our bunk houses started to fade. We'd been drinking and talking about big ideas. It wasn't anything spe-cial; we were always talking about big ideas, politics, change, who we wanted to be in the world. He was sitting on a low wall that marked the edge of lawn just past the bomb shelter. From there, a footpath led out to the apple orchards. Evan took my hand, pulled me onto his lap, and kissed me.

Nothing happened, I felt nothing. He tried again. It was not working. I waited for some kind of fire to start and then he looked at me in a way that made me laugh. "I'm sorry," he said, "It's like I'm kissing my sister."

"I know." I leaned back a little to look at him.

"I could probably keep going but I'd feel like an asshole."

I was blindsided with sadness. Evan was a great guy, smart and funny and kind and he liked me for who I was. He liked that I read books. He was impressed with the speed at which I acquired new Hebrew words. He did not find my braininess intimidating or boring. He liked me because I was odd. Because I liked books, because he often found me parked in a corner with my nose in a battered Ray Bradbury science fiction paperback, or a Stephen King thriller. He liked me because I was curious about the world we were in. When we talked about politics and history, he never made me feel small for asking questions. It seemed like no one—besides Ian and Mackey back home—had liked me for who I really was before. The boys who gave me attention now saw me like Dave did. Or they looked at me like those Israeli soldiers, like I was a package to be opened. Evan was probably the first boy who saw more of me than just the outside. He was interested in what my brain was doing, and he thought that part was the best part.

It was so complicated, figuring all this out. A boy could like me for my looks, but it didn't mean much, or a boy could like me because I was smart, but we would never be more than friends. In that moment before he kissed me, Evan seemed to like all of me. But after he kissed me, it didn't feel right. It wasn't going to be like that.

I got off Evan's knee and sat down next to him. "I really like you, Evan," I said. I was being an adult in a way I did not know I had in me. "But I want us to be friends. I don't want things to be weird." I lit a cigarette and we passed it back and forth, sitting in the dark. Light and music and conversation from the bunk houses spilled into the empty spaces between us.

"Good," said Evan, "because I want that too."

"I feel sad," I confessed. Evan was already my friend; someone I could trust. I knew it in that moment.

"I know. I know. You're awesome, you know that, right?" Evan told me about his plans for Berkeley—he was going to study something science-y. I told him I did not know what I wanted to do at all. "You're so good with language," he said. "And you're curious. Political science."

"I don't know what that even is," I said. We sat in silence for a while. "I'm thinking I might stay after this is over. Things at home are . . . I'm not ready for college and I couldn't get in anyway. I don't have the grades. I like learning Hebrew."

Evan looked at me. "I think that's a good idea," he said.

I stood up and pulled him off the wall where we'd been sitting. He wrapped his arms around me, and we stayed there for a minute before walking back up into the lights to rejoin the party.

The next day I told Dave to knock it off. I wasn't going to be with him, and he needed to get out of my way, please. A shadow crossed his face. I looked at him, perhaps for the first time, and thought about his feelings. Maybe he really did have a crush on me? I dismissed the idea out of hand. Impossible.

Telling Dave to knock it off made me feel strong. He left me alone and soon, Eli, one of the soldiers, threw himself into a chair across the table from me at every single meal. Every day when I walked past him on the porch, he'd call me over to talk, teach me to swear in Hebrew, tell me about Shabbat dinner with his family. After a few days of looking at him over my cafeteria tray, after a few nights of making out with him down in the orchards just beyond the reach of the porch lights, I was a sloppy mess of hormones.

I let Eli take me home to Haifa to meet his mother.

Eli had olive skin, black hair, and large brown eyes that always had dark circles under them. His sleepy look was impossibly sexy, as was the half-smile that appeared on his face whenever he saw me. He could not wait to show me off to his friends, to introduce me to his family. "My American," he called me, like I was some kind of rare dog breed. Eli's mom, Nila, was Persian. She's where Eli got his color from. Leo, his dad, was German, the son of Holocaust survivors. Eli had two younger brothers. They were gorgeous too; dark-skinned and dark-eyed, with that same sleepy smile I could see on their brother's face. They were taller than he was and spoke better English than he did, and they teased me like a sister from the moment we met. I could see their delight every time Eli walked in the door holding my hand. Not long after that first visit, Nila asked me to call her Ima, Hebrew for mom. So I did.

Only Leo was not sold on me. He was a big, barrel-shaped man with a white mustache and thinning white hair. He had strong arms and took up space. He was convinced there was something wrong with me. Why else would I have been sent away? I was too young for this nonsense, kibbutz or no kibbutz. Was I mentally ill, hiding a chronic disease? Something about me was not right. Eli would recount his parents' conversations, how they asked him to explain why a young girl like me was so far from home, so far from my family.

"There's nothing wrong with her," Nila would insist. She had my back. I wondered if it was from living with all these men in such a small space. She seemed so happy to have a girl around. We struggled to communicate, but somehow, it worked. I stumbled my way through conversations, she was patient with my efforts, and it felt like we had an understanding.

"She's fine," Nila said, over and over.

"But why is she here?" Leo would respond. "Who sends their kids away like this? She's too young." If he had asked me directly, I would not have had a good answer. What was I doing here, anyway? I'd spent the last two years faking it through high school. I had no plan, no obvious future. I wasn't looking to be a young mother, I didn't have a calling to join the Jewish homeland, and I wasn't built to be a farmer. Why didn't my family want me?

I worried Leo could see me, really see me. I worried he was right. I worried he knew the weaknesses in my body, and maybe worse, the weaknesses in my character. I worried he could see my love for books and words would never make me strong enough for the world. I was afraid to ask Leo about where he'd come from. I imagined that he looked at me and saw the faces of girls in his past, a past I didn't want to consider. "Something is wrong with her," he would insist. Eli told me his father would not stop chewing on the idea that I was somehow broken. "My mom loves you, though."

Their apartment was a modest living room, two bedrooms, and a tiny kitchen halfway up a boxy high rise. There was one bathroom. When I stayed over, the younger brothers would sleep on the couch and the floor in the living room. Eli and I would have silent sweaty sex in the closet-sized second bedroom while his parents slept across the hall, their door open. Field work had made me fit and Eli was in active army service. Every encounter was like competitive wrestling. It was exhausting and when we were done, we'd retreat to the narrow single beds and slap mosquitoes until we fell asleep. In the morning, we'd squeeze around the Formica-topped kitchen table for coffee and toast. Later, we'd sit in the patch of garden surrounded by a dozen identical high rises. Or we'd walk over to Eli's local café to meet his friends so he could show off his "American." When Saturday faded, we would get on the bus and go back to the kibbutz, holding hands like schoolchildren when we walked back through the gate.

Sophia did not approve of the way I let Eli treat me—like a fancy car or a new wristwatch, but I did not tell her that Eli was the same for me. He was "my Israeli." I liked having an Israeli boyfriend; I adored his mother and his sweet brothers. When I was with his family, it was easy to be different from everyone else and there was a good reason for it. I was from another country, of course I was different. There was an easy explanation for being an outsider. I was from outside. No one expected me to fit in, so unless Eli reminded me about his father's questions, I didn't worry about it.

I was Eli's shiny toy, but I think he was also genuinely proud of me. He loved helping me learn his language and I got quite good at it, fast. It was a source of endless surprise and satisfaction to find myself living in a different language and doing it well. Eli would patiently help me lead simple transactions like buying plates of hummus and cheap beer or bus tickets. He'd guide me through kitchen table conversations with his mom or help me explain to his friends what kind of work I did back on the kibbutz.

Eli grew up speaking Arabic and Hebrew, so he was no stranger to language himself. He thrived in talking to strangers, no matter where they were from. He wore the uniform of an Israeli soldier, but his attitude was that anyone we met was his neighbor. He was just as open with the Arabs and Palestinians as he was with the Israelis— and he really wanted me to love his country. Maybe he was just an accessory to my reinvention tour, maybe I was just a prestigious toy he'd acquired, but being with him was fun.

Back on the kibbutz, the soldiers would tease us for our tourist-level commitment to Israel. But I was no longer an easy mark, not with Eli at my side, not with my sassy Hebrew comebacks. And the punk Germans, those displaced adults who were waiting for something to change so they could go home? I felt that too, a sharpening of my edges, a waiting for something different, more directed. The tether that connected to my California past had been weak the day my plane left the ground and now, thanks to neglect, it had frayed close to breaking. My wardrobe had collapsed to sand boots, two pairs of shorts, a pair of jeans, and some ragged t-shirts. I'd accidentally left my one good dress behind in a hostel after an overnight with the youth group. I had a t-shirt with the name of the kibbutz on it and another one that said "Cola-Cola" in Hebrew, both baked thin from the sun. I'd given much of my stuff from home to the teenaged kids on the kibbutz. I didn't need any of it.

The summer rolled away from us and everyone grew quieter in the evenings as it came closer to time for us to go home. Evan and I still talked, but he had hooked up with Jules and they disappeared into the darkness together. I was leaving the kibbutz with Eli on Friday afternoons to spend Shabbat with his family in Haifa. I felt a twist of jealousy when I saw Evan with Jules, their heads bent together in serious conversation. But Jules was smart and kind and I mostly got over it. I wondered if Evan had told her about what happened between us, but it was nothing, nothing at all, really. And then I decided I hoped he had not. It was something to me, because Evan had seen me as something good, and I didn't want Jules to have it.

I was spending all my free time with Eli. He had been assigned to a different security detail on a different kibbutz, so I took the bus alone to Haifa on Shabbat. Sometimes, I'd get there before Eli did. I'd sit in the kitchen eating baklava with his mom while we tried to talk to each other. I would head back to the kibbutz as late as possible on Saturday nights, quietly fold myself into my bunk, and join my work crew in the fields at sunrise on Sunday morning.

I was strong from work and felt stupidly brave from living through the intermittent shelling from over the Lebanese border, as though my survival had anything to do with me. Once, we had to scramble for a bunker while we were working in the apple orchards. We were dragging ladders between the rows, plucking blossoms off the trees so the fruit would have room to grow. It was hot and dry; the sky was that relentless pale blue. Then, a streak of white smoke across the sky. The farm lead gathered us like sheep into a nearby concrete trench and we waited, practicing our newest Hebrew words. It felt like nothing more than a break. We sat with our backs leaned up against the thick walls until the all-clear siren blew. I was never afraid of the rockets, even when I could see the smoke in the sky, or a plume of dust in the distance when a rocket hit the ground and exploded. The Israelis were unflappably calm whenever the sirens went off. They never acted scared or rushed off to the shelter. Each bombing was like, I don't know, hitting traffic when you were supposed to be somewhere. You'd be late, it was annoying, maybe you had to take a detour, but that was about it. Of course, I believed I was safe, nothing around me told me otherwise.

I called home after the shelling had become a regular event. Placing a call was a huge hassle. You had to arrange it with the operator at the phone office by the cafeteria. The kibbutz operator would get the international operator on the line, place the call, and then you would wait in the phone booth in the hall while the local operator patched you through. When the call was over, you would give your hard-earned shekels to the operator—who did not want to be there because it was evening and that's when there were movies or television—to pay for the time you were on the line.

"We're fine," I told my dad. Not "I'm fine," but "We're fine." Like I was part of this place now.

"I sort of figured," he said.

"I'm thinking about staying," I said.

There was a pause. I counted how many shekels his silence would cost me as I waited for his response. "There's a lot going on here. It might not be the worst idea," he finally said.

"Can you tell Mom I'm okay? I wrote but I think it takes a long time and the bombing had just started then. It seems like it's over. Mostly. I don't know. We're fine."

"Your letters are great," Dad said. "Let me know what you decide to do, okay?"

We said goodbye and I hung up the phone. I sat in the phone box for a while. I pictured what my life would be if I were at home. Me and Ian and Mackey driving around aimlessly. All the hours spent smoking weed and listening to music. The weird tension with my dad and stepmom. I didn't want any of it.

I went to find Evan. "Will you write to me?" I asked him.

Evan and Jules had both extended their trip. They were going to travel around the country together for a few weeks. Jules had been planning to go the Hebrew University in Jerusalem all along. She was going to study history. Evan would go home after she had been assigned a dorm room. He was going to miss his first week of classes, but he was in love, so he didn't care, and he was smart enough to catch up.

"Of course, I will," Evan said.

"No, I mean it. People always say they're going to write, and they don't. Promise me you'll write to me."

"I will. I mean it. I promise."

There's this thing—it's now called a "birthright tour," but the idea isn't as new as the name. If I hadn't dropped out of Sunday school, I probably would have heard about it back then. Jewish kids go to Israel for a season, a summer, a few weeks. That's what my kibbutz summer program was. Kids in their late teens, very early twenties go to Israel, do farm work, live at a place that's basically a commune, and get exposed to a Jewish society. The birthright tour is supposed instill a sort of Jewish nationalism in you, to make you into the next generation of Zionists, the people who want to build and sustain the Jewish state. There are other kinds of trips, ones that are more about sightseeing or about studying religion. My group did a lot of sightseeing, and sometimes we had a shorter work week so we could go on field trips. But mostly my group was about kibbutz, these small communities that were supposed to teach us new ways of living on the land as a tribe. By covering our hands in the pale sandy dirt, we were meant to feel like the land was ours. Ultimately, the idea was to connect you to the State of Israel, no matter what kind of trip you were on.

It would be easy to say that this propaganda program worked on me. I appeared to be a perfect success story. A nice Jewish girl comes from California and decides to continue her time in Eretz Yisrael, the land of Israel. She works the land, learns the language, finds an Israeli partner, and joins the tribe. That's one way to look at it.

There's another way to look at it. It was not that I wanted to stay. It was that I didn't feel like I had anywhere else to go. Israel wanted me like nowhere else did, not even my own family.

"There must be something wrong with her," Eli's dad insisted. I could hear him talking in the room across the hall in the tiny Haifa apartment. "Why wouldn't her family want her home?"

CHAPTER SIX:
Language Lessons

My volunteer group had a bittersweet last night, gathering on the lawn, trading addresses and hugs. Evan promised again he'd write to me. The bus left for the airport at dawn, but we were all used to the early wake up calls, to the coffee and dry biscuits. I said goodbye to Lauren, and I was genuinely sorry to see her go. She cried and hugged me again before she got on the bus; I waved as it pulled away. I knew Evan would be sharing his empty room with Jules, so I sat on my bed reading, waiting for Eli to come get me.

Eli and I had a plan. He was on leave for a few weeks. We would find a place for me to enroll in Hebrew school. Then we would hitchhike south into the Sinai, where we'd sleep on the beach until my classes started or Eli had to sign back into service, whichever came first.

Finding a work-study program was easy. The same agency that organized my tour had an office in Tel Aviv. I picked up the phone at Eli's house and called them. They sent the paperwork and Eli helped me pick a place close to Haifa where he lived. It would be just like my last kibbutz but with a formal language program. Students worked morning shifts with the other volunteers and, four afternoons a week, had Hebrew classes. We would have Friday afternoons and all day

Saturday off. I would work to pay for my room, board, and education. I'd get a small stipend—beer and cigarette money, money for bus trips into town on my days off. I still had some traveler's checks left, too. Over the course of the summer, there'd been so little for me to spend my money on. I'd be fed, housed, get paid, and learn a language. As a bonus, I had a gorgeous Israeli boyfriend who lived in town, a short bus ride away. Travel first, a beach vacation, then school. It sounded perfect.

I ditched what few extra things I had at Eli's place in Haifa. At dawn, we walked out to the highway to hitch nearly 400 miles to Dahab, a rugged kibbutz village on the edge of the Red Sea. Getting rides wasn't difficult. Eli wore his military gear and I was a teenage girl—people stopped. We were traveling light, two small daypacks and two sleeping bags. We got our first ride right away, and then our second. We were never on the roadside for long. We got in and out of military trucks, throwing our bags in the back. Eli would put me in the middle and throw his arm around my shoulders. He'd charm each driver with his easy manner, with his stories, and he'd introduce me like a prize: his American girlfriend. By dusk that same day, we were unrolling our sleeping bags on the sand under the palm trees, the Sinai Mountains a shadow behind us, the Red Sea whispering in front of us.

Sinai was a mostly barren wedge of land between Jordan, Egypt, and Israel. It was all pale earth and scrub plants with a mountain range in the middle where supposedly Moses had received the Ten Commandments from God. Israel and Egypt had been battling for control of Sinai since 1967, in no small part because the Suez Canal, at the top end of the Egyptian side of the wedge, was a major channel for international shipping. In 1979 the two countries signed a peace treaty. The land would eventually all go back to Egypt. It was in transition when I was there. The Israelis were gradually shutting things down, dismantling their army bases, closing down a few tough desert farming co-ops. In the meantime, religious pilgrims on Holy Land tours were still venturing inland to the site of Moses' burning bush while divers and no-frills travelers would eat popsicles on the shore and explore the vibrant reef just below the surface of the Red Sea.

We spent a week camping on the beach. Maybe it was ten days, time didn't matter. Most of the time, Eli was stripped down to nothing but his sandals. The beach was an even strip of sand with palm trees here and there, the sharp leaves casting equally sharp outlines onto the pale ground. The nearby kibbutz had a small shop, a café, and freshwater showers for campers and beachgoers who got tired of being crusted with salt. The kibbutz rented campsites and had hostel-style bunks, but there was no need for formal camping. It was so dry; there was zero chance of rain. It was too dry for mosquitoes and it was never cold. And it was safe. We didn't think twice about leaving our things unattended while we swam. At night, the only light came from the perimeter of the kibbutz and the pinholes the stars punched in the black blanket of the sky.

There was a nomadic Bedouin population in the Sinai, Arabic speakers who had lived in the desert for ages. Bedouin boys would walk down the beach selling strong Turkish coffee and warm fire-charred flat bread. The men would slowly drive across the sand in their Mercedes sedans, collecting a few shekels from anyone who wanted to rent a palm leaf shack for privacy. Sometimes they had ice chests filled with cold beer and bottled water in their trunks of their fancy cars.

Eli always made time to talk to the Bedouins. They were covered head to toe in their black robes and kaffiyeh. Eli would stand there, naked but for his sandals, one hand on the fender of a big sedan, laughing with the Bedouin men like they were his brothers. Once or twice a day Eli would pull on his shorts and wander off, leaving me to read a Vonnegut novel or a battered Agatha Christie mystery—whatever book I'd managed to scrounge off other travelers—with my back up against a palm tree. I'd hear the crunch of his sandals and look up when he called my name or some Hebrew term of affection. "Hey, chamoudi, sweetie." He'd stand in front of me with that big sleepy smile, his hands full with chewy pita sandwiches stuffed with grilled vegetables, the tahini sauce making the paper wrapper stick to the bread. He'd make a cold beer appear from the side pocket of his cargo shorts. Sometimes he brought ice cream too.

During the day, we'd wander into the warm waters of the Red Sea, walking in the shallows to spot the bright tropical fish. Eli might appear with a mask and snorkel. "I borrowed it from that guy, over there." He would point down the beach with his chin. "Thank you!" he'd shout, and a silhouette of a person would wave our direction. I'd pull on a t-shirt to keep the sun off my back while I floated above the shallow reef, hypnotized by all the life just below the surface of the water.

After dark we'd crash into each other until we were worn out, then we'd lie on the sand listening to the surf until we fell asleep. I was enchanted. I wanted nothing, nothing at all. When it came time for me to go back north to school, for Eli to report back to the army, I dragged my feet as we walked to the highway at dawn.

We hitched back north to Haifa easily. At one point we shoehorned ourselves into the tiny cargo space in the back of a two seated convertible, clinging to the flattened rag top, our bags smashed under the front passenger's feet. The driver had the radio playing at full volume. "He's crazy!" Eli said to me, and whacked the driver on the shoulder, laughing. It was completely unsafe, but we returned to Haifa with no damage, just a coating of road dust and sunburn. We did laundry while Eli's mom fed us and fed us and fed us again. A few days later, Eli borrowed a car and took me to the place that would be my next home.

I fell in love with Ronnie, my roommate, right away. She was from Boston and had an East Coast accent. She was tall with short dark hair and big brown eyes. She was older than me but didn't condescend. She was the best girlfriend and big sister I didn't know I'd been missing. She was studying anthropology but had taken a term off to learn Hebrew. She was a self-declared feminist, but she liked boys, she really liked boys. She talked openly about sex like it was something everyone did and no one needed to be freaked out about. Ronnie and I were fast inseparable. We shared clothes and books and went on weekend adventures together when Eli was on duty.

It was harvest season and much of the work was in the citrus orchards picking grapefruits and oranges. We'd walk down the rows of fragrant trees wearing canvas kangaroo pouch bags. You would pick the fruit with a twist of your hand and drop it in the bag, and then, when the bag was full—but not too heavy—you'd open the bottom of it and gently pour the fruit out into big plastic crates. The orchards were beautiful, bright yellow and green and orange under the blue skies. We'd come back from the fields smelling of sweat and citrus peel, our fingers coated in the waxy paste left behind from handling so much fruit. I liked the weird leggy ladders, so tall and so light, and the round noise the fruit made when it tumbled into the crates. I liked the shiny leaves and pungent scent of unripe oranges.

There was always a tinny boom box playing the radio somewhere, on the hood of the tractor, perched on the corner of the big plastic bins. Ofra Haza's voice drifted into the sky. Or maybe it was Blondie singing Rapture and someone singing along would screw up the rap part, and everyone would laugh. The harvest mattered, it mattered that we got the work done, but it never felt rushed. There were plenty of breaks to sit in the shade dunking biscuits in a plastic mug of lukewarm coffee. The days were easy—field work in the mornings, lunch, and then Hebrew class until most of the kibbutz settled into lazy late afternoon napping for the hottest part of the day.

Eli called me regularly, leaving messages at the phone office, letting me know when he'd be off duty and when he could visit. Sometimes he'd show up and Ronnie would find somewhere else to be so we could be alone. On holidays and weekends, I'd take the bus to Haifa and stay with Eli and his family. The apartment would fill with Nila's boys, laughing and noisy and sweet. And Leo would come home from work, questioning my presence with his pale blue eyes. I was happy; it was weird.

Eli finished up his military service and I should have seen it coming, but I was still so naïve. It was his turn to take off to see the world, to go wandering before he did whatever was next. Finding a grown-up job, going to university, I don't even know. We never talked about the future. He had planned to leave Israel for six weeks to travel around Europe. I went to see him off with his brother and his best friend.

I cried when we said goodbye, tears spilling down my face, my throat sore, my heart hot and tight under my ribs. The blue-black wall of the ferry hull towered over us.

"This was just supposed to be for fun," Eli said, wiping the tears from my cheeks. "Look at you."

I tried to smile, but I was heartbroken. Eli was my first real boy-friend. He made me feel like I was special but not weird. It wasn't just the sex, though with Eli it was different. I understood there was sup-posed to be something in it for me, too. He wanted me, no one had wanted me like that before, but also, he openly talked about me as his girlfriend. He wanted people to know we were together. I could not believe this charismatic, good-looking young man cared about me. He looked at me like I was worth something and he made me believe it. I had fallen in love.

I was so embarrassed; my feelings were right on the surface where everyone could see them. Eli stepped back, shouldered his pack, and boarded the ship for Athens. We watched him go up the gangplank, and then lost sight of him. The boys looked at me awkwardly while I stared at my feet to hide my face. Eli's brother broke the silence. "Come on," he said, "we'll take you home."

We didn't talk while we waited for the bus. Eli's brother put his arm around me, like he was my brother, not Eli's, and I felt better. They both rode with me back to the kibbutz and walked me to the gate. "You'll still come for Shabbat," Eli's brother said. "Just because Eli's gone doesn't mean you can skip Friday dinner." I promised; I meant it. Then they crossed the street and hitchhiked back to Haifa.

Even with Eli gone, I looked forward to bouncing up the stairs to his family's apartment. I never called ahead but they expected me all the same. I would roll a clean shirt into my day pack and wander out to the bus stop on the two-lane road. It wasn't far to town, about an hour to the bus station, with all the local stops. I tried to time my visits to Haifa so I could get falafel at the takeout counter in the bus station. I'd arrive around lunchtime. After I paid, I'd stuff my sand-wich with pickles and slather it in extra sauce, then find a bench where I could eat and watch the people: Israeli soldiers in uniform, girls and boys, rifles over their shoulders. Arab women in body obscuring black dresses with white headscarves, their arms hefting shopping bags full of produce. American tourists like me, barely adults, wearing college sweatshirts and practicing their clunky Hebrew at the bus ticket window. I'd toss the falafel wrapper, wash the tahini sauce off my hands, and take the short walk to the cluster of apartment buildings where Eli's family lived.

I loved arriving to find that Nila had just taken the baklava out of the oven. She would ask me about my week, about my classes. She would slice the corner piece of pastry out of the pan and give it to me on a small white plate with a glass of sweet hot tea. She would show me the postcards Eli sent home and read them out loud—my spoken language had improved remarkably, but reading was still hard. Once Nila told me that Eli had called, and he had asked about me. I missed him tremendously, but not for a minute did it occur to me that once his six weeks were over, we would not pick up where we left off.

Sometimes I skipped Shabbat and Ronnie and I would explore, booking ourselves into cheap hostels, wandering Israel's ancient cities, working out our Hebrew lessons in less forgiving environments than the kibbutz, where everyone knew we were students. We went swimming in the Sea of Galilee and stayed in a hostel in Tiberias, a small city that was mostly ancient ruins with a few newer hotels along the waterfront. We took long walks along the golden walls around the oldest parts of Jerusalem. We bought beaded brass earrings and scarves from flirtatious Arabs in the narrow alleys of the market, young men who'd call after us. "Just come look, I have tea, come look, drink tea and talk! No pressure!" We got hit on everywhere we went, and it was mostly harmless. Once we ended up eating a late-night dinner with some boys who insisted we needed to come back to their place and eat their mom's hummus. And we did, and we ended up eating hummus, really, before walking back to our hostel in the dark.

I told Ronnie we had to take time off to visit Sinai, as though the transfer of that land back to Egypt was going to make it disappear. It was the freest place I'd ever been; I wanted to share it with my new best friend. We hitchhiked down to Sinai, just like Eli and I had done, splitting up to ride with two guys who were driving military convoy vehicles down into the desert. One of the guys was fine, perfectly well mannered, but when we swapped halfway through the journey, I learned that the other guy had been hitting on Ronnie the whole time. I did not think he would bother with me. It didn't occur to me that any girl would do for his purposes. I figured I was getting Ronnie out of a bad situation, not putting myself in one.

"Don't worry," I said to Ronnie, as I climbed into the cab of the truck.

The driver asked the usual questions—where was I from, where did I learn Hebrew, how long had I been in the country, did I want to slide over and sit right next to him?

"I'm fine right here," I said. I realized how stupid I'd been. Ronnie and I should have both climbed into the nice guy's truck. The two had a radio, they were talking back and forth and after I started to get upset, bad guy radioed nice guy and they dumped us both at a road-side checkpoint. We weren't worried about getting stuck, but I was angry.

"I'm an idiot," I said to Ronnie.

"You wanted to trust him. We were both idiots. We should have stayed together."

We stood in the dark, watching the trucks get smaller and smaller as they rolled away. We looked at the military checkpoint and walked to where the light hit the road. We had no trouble getting another ride, but we did not split up again. It was dark when we got to Dahab, but there was enough moonlight for us to find an empty palm leaf shack. We crawled in and did not wake up until the sun was high in the sky the next day.

When we peeked outside our shack, a beautiful Israeli boy with long hair in perfect corkscrew curls—why were they always so pretty?—asked us if we wanted coffee. He'd made extra and wanted absolutely nothing in return. The entire week we were there, this gorgeous boy would bring us coffee every morning. We would return the glasses an hour later, thank him, and go swimming in the clear waters of the Red Sea.

CHAPTER SEVEN:
No More Baklava

I ironed laundry. I washed dishes. I learned how to drive a cherry-picker, an awkward mustard colored zig zag shaped machine with a lift you stand on so you could reach the fruit high in the trees. The kibbutz had dozens of jobs, and I did everything I was assigned to do. I worked morning shifts, ate lunch, and went to class. Under fluorescent lights I learned to conjugate my verbs, to write the swirly Hebrew letters used in cursive, to describe my work and my family and my home. In the evenings I sat on the steps of our two-story building and drank cheap beer, peeling the Maccabee brand labels off bottles wet with condensation. I read the *Jerusalem Post*, smoked cigarettes, and talked bullshit with my classmates.

Two weeks went by, then four, and one day someone came to get me to tell me I had a phone call.

Eli was home.

I took the next day off and sat on the stairs until Eli appeared in front of my building. I was nervous. Ronnie was at work, so I stuck a note on the door and locked it behind me. We would have had a few hours. We stripped off our clothes and got in the shower, and then, we lay in bed talking. Eli told me everywhere he'd been, France and

Spain and Germany and . . . I'd received a few letters in English. He told me he'd had help writing them. He looked at me and paused.

"There were girls," he said. "One in France, and two in Spain and . . . I did not forget about you."

I sat up and pulled away from him. "You should go," I said.

"I did not forget about you," he said, trying again.

"You should go. It's still early enough for you to get a bus, you won't have to hitchhike. You can be home in time for dinner. Say hi to your mom for me."

In that moment, I was not angry, I did not cry. I felt flat, two-dimensional. Eli looked confused, like he could not quite believe this was happening. I guess I was supposed to be okay with this honesty. I was supposed to say we were not exclusive, and we'd just go back to how we were before. But the spell had been broken. All this time I felt like I'd been special to Eli. It was ruined when he stacked me next to his other acquisitions. I was just another girl.

"Eli, go home," I said for the last time.

Eli got dressed, pulling on his army-issued cargo pants, his khaki T-shirt, his sandals. I watched him, feeling a little dizzy. It was like I was watching this happen to someone else. How could he be so cruel? He looked at me expectantly, like if he waited long enough, I'd say something different. But I was done. I opened the door and time slowed down, almost stopped. He shook his head at me and headed for the front gate. I lit a cigarette and sat on the steps of the building, watching until he was out of sight. A few days later, the calls started. Once or twice a week I would get a message from the office. A scrawled note with Eli's name and phone number.

It was week three when Eli's mom called. I went to the phone box to take the call. "I wish you'd come and see us," she said.

"I really miss visiting with you," I told her. It was true. I missed Eli's brothers and Shabbat dinner. I even missed Eli's dad trying to figure me out. I missed sitting with Nila on Friday afternoons, waiting for her boys to come home. I missed her saving the corner of her homemade baklava for me. I missed her asking me about my week. I missed Eli, too, and the way he made me feel when we were first together.

"He told me about the girls. He said you were mad." She paused. "Maybe you could come and see us."

"I'm sorry, Nila, I really am," I said. "I just can't."

I don't know what I expected. When Eli told me he had been with other girls, I was hardly surprised. Of course he was fucking his way across Europe. He was good looking and funny and charming. He made friends everywhere. But why did he need to tell me? What was he trying to say by listing his hookups along with the names of the countries he'd been to visit? Was he trying to clear his conscience? Was he showing me his souvenirs? What was the point?

That anger I should have felt when he told me about the girls took its time to reach me. It arrived with a lot of sadness. I'd fallen in love not just with Eli, but with his family. He'd ruined it with this laundry list of one-night stands. I couldn't let it go. I didn't want to be the kind of person who just let it go. We had made no promises, so he hadn't really cheated on me. But I felt cheated on all the same.

I hung up the phone and walked back to my room. Ronnie was sitting on the steps drinking beer. It was a warm evening, the sky was clear. Ronnie pushed her cigarettes over to me and I told her about the call. I had already told her about Eli listing the girls like stamps in his passport. I was so embarrassed; like it was something I'd done wrong, not him. I repeated the story, and she just listened, even though she'd heard it a dozen times already.

"I wish I had not . . . I mean, we did it in the shower and then he told me everything. Why did we not talk first?"

"It's okay," said Ronnie. "Biology is weird. Sex makes people crazy. It's normal. You didn't know. How would you know? Also, Eli's hot. I don't blame you. Consider it your last ride."

I laughed. She always had some story for me about making mistakes and feeling stupid about it. But she gave herself plenty of room to screw up. She would take a deep breath and tell herself not to do it again. And she didn't blame herself for some guy who treated her like crap. He was the asshole. He was the one who should have behaved better.

"His mom made really good baklava," I said.

She rolled her eyes. "This is Israel," she said. "That shit is everywhere."

I was surrounded by a community of young adults who had time on their hands, lots of freedom, and few inhibitions. Of course sex was a thing. But I feel like no one ever told me about sex. I mean, there's your standard making babies stuff, and there's the mechanics of it, but that's all so basic. Sex—straight sex, I mean—was something boys did to girls. You were either doing it or you weren't. We did not talk about our expectations for it or how you'd know if you were doing it right or how it was supposed to make you feel. It was almost like a sport, something you did with your body, like swimming or taking a bike ride. We worried about getting pregnant and the weird diseases you could get, but my friends did not talk about how it could be fun or how it could kind of fuck you up if you weren't clear about your feelings. Because birth control was so easy to get, we had all the freedom to have sex with whomever we wanted. But no one ever told me how it could be like drugs—tilting the ground, messing with your brain, making you feel things that you couldn't quite explain or control.

In addition to the language students, my new kibbutz also housed two dozen or so European workers. They were mostly British, with a few Swedish girls who were just looking for a cheap vacation and a good time. Unlike with the Germans at my first kibbutz, the American students and the British workers were friendly with each other. And it was a common topic of conversation in the evenings, which American had been seen going back to which British worker's bunk. Everyone was hooking up; I was no exception. I wasn't very smart about it though, and Trevor, the English guy I ended up with, was a very bad choice.

Trevor had a live-in girlfriend, Lotte, from Denmark. She was tall and freckled and had long straight red hair. She was gorgeous and looked like a swimsuit model. Trevor told me she was frigid; I did not know what this meant. I interpreted this as meaning she did not like sex. Trevor told me they had a deal: he could do it with whomever he wanted as long as he was not a jerk about it. I wanted to believe he was telling the truth. It's how I justified my behavior.

I don't remember how it started, I just remember that one evening Trevor was in my room asking me to do things I had not done before and making red and sore in places where I had not been red and sore before. It happened over and over and over again. I'd spend a few hours with Trevor, and then walk around lightheaded for days, thinking about his sandy hair and his amused expression and his British vowels. Every time Trevor touched me, my brain liquefied, and it would take hours for me to focus again. I guess I knew sex was supposed to be fun, but in an academic sort of way, like I knew my

Walkman was made in a factory in Japan. And I guess it was fun with Eli, but this was super hot. Maybe it's because deep down I knew we were doing something wrong and it was thrilling or maybe it was something else. I was on fire when we were together. Trevor knew what he wanted, and he would tell me, and then I would forget everything. I was drunk on sex, and that made me believe everything Trevor said. Plus, Lotte, she was kind of cold; no one liked her. Maybe it was true what Trevor said. I wanted to believe I was not hurting anyone, not really. I wanted to believe it was no big deal; it was just, you know, sex.

We were doing a terrible job of keeping it discreet. The kibbutz had a common room, a sort of shared living room, where we'd go after dinner and watch the news on TV or read the paper. The common room was always open for coffee and snacks, there were always people hanging out, always someone to talk to.

I'd sit with Ronnie and Brian, a stocky guy from Texas. Ronnie had hooked up with Brian for reasons I couldn't quite understand. She told me it was just sex, and because I was pretending that's why I was with Trevor, I acted like I understood. Ronnie and Brian were friends, though. They talked, they laughed, and they behaved like they were boyfriend and girlfriend.

Trevor and I did not act like we were friends; we didn't hang out like Ronnie and Brian did. I'd sit with my American classmates; he'd be on the opposite side of the room with Lotte and the English workers. He'd look at me and mouth something obscene. He'd lick his fingers like no one else was watching. I would flush hot, get up, and walk out. Minutes later he'd be running to catch up with me; putting his hands in my hair and making me feel confused. I wanted what he was doing, and it made me feel bad all at once. But when Trevor would pull me into the shadows behind a building on a hot night, I forgot Lotte existed.

Crating chickens was the worst job on the kibbutz. It took place at night because the chickens were calmer, or so they told us. Everyone had to be there: the whole farm, the volunteers, and the residents. It was an all hands on deck kind of activity. There was no getting out of it without some kind of medical excuse.

The chicken houses held seemingly thousands of fat white birds. On packing night, a crew would set up a conveyer belt in front of the coop. On one end, a stack of crates, on the other end, a truck. Once the doors of the coop were open, one of the men would drive a little front loader into a sea of panicked birds, scoop up the chickens in the bucket, and dump them in a mound in a temporary enclosure with a low fence around it. We had to reach in, grab the chickens by the legs, and stuff them headfirst into the crates. We'd push the crates full of screaming birds to the end of the belt where they'd be stacked on the truck. Feathers and bird shit were everywhere. The chickens squawked like crazy; the coop was full of bright lights and engine noise from the loader. It was chaos. Calmer at night. Not even.

The second worst job was working the potato harvester, a monster of a machine that scraped off the top layer off the potato fields. The machine threw the dirt at you while you tossed rocks and plants and things that were not potatoes off the side. I couldn't work on the harvester. Every time I tried, I was blinded with snot and tears and dust. I couldn't see, I couldn't breathe. Still, working up on that noisy, dirty machine was nowhere near as bad as boxing chickens. Potatoes were not live animals—you could not hear their legs or wings break when you grabbed them. They did not scratch you with their beaks and claws. They did not squawk at you in fear or cover you in shit and blood and feathers.

Crating chickens took a few hours, or until the coop was empty, whichever came first. The shifts were short but felt like they would never end. When it was over, it was a race for the showers. The climate was so mild most of the time, hot water hardly ever mattered. But after boxing chickens, you wanted a hot shower. You wanted to scrub every inch of yourself with soap and water as hot as you could stand.

One night after crating birds, I was in the women's shower house scrubbing bird shit and feathers from my hair, soaping up the scratches on my arms. Lotte was the first person to come in after me. "Leave some for the rest of us," she barked at me in her clipped Danish accent.

I clenched my jaw and hoped someone, anyone, would come in after her. I did not want to be alone with her for even a minute. I was hot with guilt and shame. "Don't use all the hot water," she said again.

"Just finishing up," I chirped and tried not to look at her. I was still so young, bony, and small. She stood there naked, all freckles and perfect long curves, so much like what I imagined an adult woman should look like. I felt like trash. What was the matter with me? I turned off the water, wrapped myself in a towel and fled.

I couldn't look Trevor in the eye after that night. Lotte's freckled arms, covered in scratches just like mine, her high, smooth forehead speckled with bird shit, none of it could erase the fact that this woman—I was just a girl—was beautiful and very strong and I did not want to fuck with her. She was not going to fight me, but she could have, and she would have won. Trevor had to be lying. He was awful to her, but she would not be humiliated by me, this stick of a not-even-adult American girl. I was just an easy acquisition for Trevor, another object for his collection. He could add me to his lists of souvenirs, like one of Eli's girls while he was traveling. There was a French girl, a Spanish girl . . . and earlier, an American girl. Me.

The best job on the kibbutz was working in the avocado orchards. You spent the day rolling between the trees on a cherry picker—and it was fun. The guys who led that crew were especially good-natured, and a little bit lazy. Every morning they cooked an amazing breakfast in the harvesting shed. You had to get up early to work the avocados, really early. You'd stumble up to the cafeteria and into the back of a van in pitch darkness. But when break time came, you'd be eating avocado and cheese omelets and drinking coffee and explaining that you did not vote for Ronald Reagan to the British volunteers who never tired of winding up the Yanks, as they called us. You'd be joking with the Israelis who thought they were teaching you how to swear while passing the coffee. And then they'd teach you how to say, "Pass the coffee."

After the citrus harvest was over, I pleaded to be moved to the avocado orchards. I'd been working the laundry because I did not look strong and I spoke passable Hebrew. But I wanted to be outside. The women in the laundry were nice enough and working there helped me learn more vocabulary, but I was bored and lonely. The laundry ladies and I were polite to each other, but we were not going to be friends. I'd finally got my wish. It was like an invitation to be one of the cool kids. It's where I'd met Trevor and the rest of the British workers.

But after seeing Lotte in the showers, I asked to be moved to a night job. Suddenly, I wanted to be alone, away from the rest of the volunteers. The kibbutz had a metal production factory—they made plumbing parts and heating vents and I don't know what else. It had two shifts daily, and I asked for the later shift.

There was an American guy in his twenties who had moved from the US to Israel permanently. He worked the second shift with me. He taught me how to work the pipe threader, then he worked the metal press a few machines over. The night crew was small; it was often just the two of us on the shop floor. We would turn up the radio and sing along with whatever the Voice of America broadcast was playing. "Stars shining bright above you," we'd sing, if it was oldies hour, or "I can feel it coming in the air tonight," which was always on, over and over, or "Don't stop believing" which sounded like California. Every night I'd end up coated in machine oil, tiny nicks in my hands from metal shavings. But it wasn't boxing chickens and I didn't have to look anyone in the eye. While I was feeling guilty and stupid and lost, I preferred the factory, even though the work was dirty, and it was hard to scrub away the smell of machine oil. I could listen to the radio and think. I didn't see anyone until lunch time most days.

My Hebrew classes were coming to an end. In October 1981, Anwar Sadat, the president of Egypt, was assassinated. I had no idea what this meant for the country, but the Israelis we worked with were trading their blue work-shirts for olive green, shouldering weapons, and heading out the gate. There were a lot of shifts open because of the mobilization. I worked the jobs no one wanted. Second shifts in the factory. Afternoons in the laundry, when everyone was sleeping off the early morning. The kitchen staffed by old ladies in house coats with numbers tattooed on their arms. They were silent and serious. They'd give me a task and leave me to it. I did not like working with them—the weight of their history scared me. I asked to be moved again, and I worked the big industrial dishwasher, rinsing plates and pans with the metal sprayer and loading them on a conveyer belt.

The dishwasher station was steamy and noisy and like working in a sauna. Even on the hottest days, it felt good to go stand on the back steps to get some fresh air. Away from kitchen ladies, with their terrifying history on their skin, I could sing along to the radio and have my own thoughts.

My Hebrew accelerated at a breakneck pace. In the weird jobs no one wanted, I was often the only volunteer. The Israelis I worked with did not even try to speak English with me. Like the soldiers at that first kibbutz who defaulted to Hebrew first, everyone assumed I knew what they were talking about. I had to ask them to slow down. I had to point at things, to try to explain with my hands when I was not understood. I was forced to learn.

I'd been in Israel less than six months, but California seemed very, very far away. I felt like those last years of high school had been erased. Or scrambled. On the surface, I acted like I was assimilating, but inside, I still felt displaced. I wasn't making friends with the Israelis I worked with. And I'd distanced myself from the other volunteers because I wasn't working with them anymore. I wanted to fit in, but I didn't know how.

CHAPTER EIGHT:
Mail Call

The mail came every evening after dinner. It didn't matter if there was something for me or not. It was still a delight to see a postcard from someone else's hometown or a brown envelope with English language magazines that I could borrow later. British gossip, music mags, anything at all to read was welcome.

I'd been getting letters from Evan—he really did write. He told me about Berkeley, how he and Jules had also spent time in Sinai before he went back home, what he missed about Israel (mostly, being outside all the time). I told him how the work was always different, how I'd just stopped talking to Eli, how things were unfolding in Israeli politics.

There was Sadat's assassination, and the return of the Sinai Peninsula to Egypt. There been bombings all summer—Israeli fighter jets on runs to southern Lebanon and Beirut, and intermittent rockets back over into Israel. The Israelis had bombed a nuclear plant in Iraq, well beyond their borders, declaring it a threat. By the end of 1981, they had claimed the disputed mountain range between Israel and Syria, the Golan Heights. And there was constant aggression between Israel and the Palestinian Liberation Organization. Israel's tiny peace activist movement would fill the news, but the government showed no interest in creating a settlement with the Palestinian people. There was so much changing all at once, and the more I understood of the language, the more I felt the low-level tension and uncertainty that seemed to be a constant part of Israeli life.

I had written to my dad about Eli, saying I had this Israeli boyfriend. I had not written about us breaking up. I had not written about the politics. In my world, Egypt and Israel and Lebanon were on the news every night. I sort of figured my dad would know about this. And even if it wasn't headline stuff at home, he would seek it out because I was there. I sort of assumed people back home would care about what was happening where I was, half a world away. A few weeks before Hebrew classes ended, I called my dad in California.

"The Sadat assassination has everyone on edge," I told him. It would have been more accurate to say that country had been on edge all along. I just hadn't connected the dots. There was an ongoing war on the border, just north of us. There were always military convoys heading towards somewhere. There were always fighter planes flying overhead so low we could see the pilots' faces, so low that we waved at them and sometimes they waved back. Israel was in a state of eternal war with its neighbors almost every day, but it was such a normal part of daily life that it didn't feel like anything unusual was happening. It only felt like there was war when we were experiencing it firsthand—sleeping in shelters, hearing the shells hit the ground, watching the explosions light up the sky.

"I'm sure you're safe," my dad said.

"I don't know what I'm going to do when classes are over. I'm thinking about staying, I guess." I wasn't lying, exactly, but I wasn't telling the truth either. I was trying the idea on for size as I said it out loud.

My classmates were going their own directions, their studies over. Ronnie was going back to college. Brian, the big Texan Ronnie had hooked up with, had gone through the Jewish Agency to find another posting on a smaller farm. That left me, a handful of Americans, and the British volunteers.

Judith was my new feminist friend. American, and another Santa Cruz lesbian like Sophia, she was big, her curly hair always pulled back behind a bandana. Whenever one of the guys would proposition me, Judith would suggest I should try sex with a woman. I thought she was just being academic, like, "You could do this other thing instead." I never believed anyone was serious, ever. I always thought they were making fun of me in some way I did not understand. I was not offended; I didn't feel harassed. It was like they were talking to me about something that had absolutely nothing to do with me. I'd get these up-front propositions. It felt like a guy was asking to use a cigarette lighter, borrow a book, get in bed to fuck for the afternoon. I couldn't tell the difference in between any them. They all had the same weight.

Judith's suggestions felt like she was offering to help out. "Hey, you should totally explore lesbian sex" was delivered in exactly the same tone as "I'm running up to the shop. Can I get you anything?" There was nothing sexy about any of it, not to me, and I was stunned when Ronnie told me something gossipy—one of the other volunteers had said I was a tease. I never initiated any of this, and I was always saying *no*, how on earth was I teasing? I had not forgotten Hannes blaming me for what happened after he climbed into my bed that night, how he acted like it was my fault he'd been send away. I was a tease; it was my fault? How?

When I told Judith about what had happened with Trevor, she stopped telling me to consider sex with women and started telling me what to read. "No self-respecting woman would be letting a guy use her like that," she said. "You need educating."

She'd rattle of the names of various authors, various manifestos I needed to get my hands on. But how was that supposed to happen? My reading diet was subject to the whims of what fellow English-speaking travelers had left behind. I was deep into Robert Graves' *I, Claudius*, the sprawling historical recounting of classical Rome. It was all sex and murder and political intrigue, and I was enthralled. I'd acquired a massive copy of *Let's Go Europe*, a guide to seeing the continent for cheap. When I was not reading Graves, I'd wonder how I was going to save enough money to get to Paris. I enjoyed Judith's thoughtful company even if I didn't have access to her reading list. Her opinionated advice was more about my being ill-equipped to respond to my situation than my making bad choices. It felt like someone cared enough to notice what I was up to and wanted to give me the tools to figure things out. I didn't have access to what she was offering me as guidelines; I appreciated them all the same.

I still didn't understand how it was always about my failings. It was so confusing. Even people who were on my side seemed to think I was the one to blame. Like a solid grounding in theoretical feminism would have kept Hannes from drunkenly falling into my bed. Like it would have kept Eli from breaking my heart or Trevor from treating me like prey. Okay, maybe it would have helped with that last one. Maybe. Ronnie was way more sensible with her "sex makes people crazy" take. She recognized that I might not be the only crazy one, that there was responsibility enough to spread around.

"I'm trying to decide if I should stay or, I don't know." I told my dad. "I have work and my Hebrew is getting really good, but I don't know what's next."

"I'm sure you'll be fine," my dad said. "It seems like things are going well for you there."

Things were not going well. I was working weird shifts that no one wanted. I'd handed my body to multiple guys who treated me as though I was an obstacle course to complete. Once they'd mastered it, I did not matter anymore. While I'd excelled at the academic part of my journey and continued to gain skill in spoken Hebrew, there was little for me to do with that skill besides fend off the ever-present attentions of Israeli boys. It was no help at all when they found my street-level Hebrew was a fair match for theirs. I'd have done better to stick with English and pretend I did not understand them.

I received a letter from my mom about the same time I put the call in to my dad. She was getting married to the man she'd been living with for a while. I liked him, and because he was nearly fifteen years younger than my mom, he understood some things about me—like that my smoking weed was mostly harmless, contrary to my mom's reefer madness take on that pastime. He liked to build things and he rode a motorcycle. We liked the some of the same music. He played records for me and talked to me about drugs in a candid way that my mom had no vocabulary for. But I did not think much of her suggesting I should see her boyfriend as my new dad. I already had a dad, as terribly flawed as he was. And she didn't invite me home to be part of their new lives. I read my mom's change of status as one less place in the world I might return to if—when—I decided to go back.

I also got a letter from my high school friend Casey. She wasn't a writer; it was a big deal to hear from her. She had gotten pregnant and had been shipped off to Idaho where it was not at all clear what was supposed to happen. She was going to have the baby, send it up for adoption, and then go to some kind of camp or reform school for difficult daughters or something.

I tried to imagine Casey resting in a dormitory with other girls who had disappointed their parents. Or going on health-bolstering walks about some summer camp-style compound not unlike the kibbutz. I tried to imagine her contained by fences and by the consequences of her mistakes. Casey could be kind of wild. She was the one who led me out on those secret late-night escapes. It still hurt, remembering that her parents thought I was the bad influence. I could not believe they blamed me for the shit she got up to. Still, I knew her mistakes were not her fault alone.

To think I had been jealous of her seemingly secure secure life. Casey's parents stayed married when everyone around us was getting divorced. She had lived at the same house with a swimming pool her whole life. Her parents bought her a car for her sixteenth birthday. She was lucky; her life seemed so even, so stable. My parents split up and I went to three high schools. Something was going on with my dad and things were always changing. I had managed to get through all this shit without getting pregnant. It made me mad that Casey seemed to have everything and fucked it up like this. I knew I was being a bad friend, but I was angry and had no idea how to answer Casey's letter. So I didn't.

"It sounds like things are going well for you," my dad had said.

My mom was getting married. My oldest friend was sent away like a ruined girl in a Victorian drama. With classes over, my best friend Ronnie was going home to Boston, back to university in time for winter classes. I still missed going to Eli's house for Shabbat, but that was not happening, no way, no how. I was mad at myself for falling for Trevor's lies about Lotte. I liked getting letters from Evan, but they reminded me of how much I had not figured out. Were things going well? I didn't understand where things were going at all. How could they be going well?

"Yeah, they think there might be a war. We don't know what's going to happen," I told him.

"That's interesting. Let me know what you decide to do," my dad said. I don't think he was listening to me. I could have said anything. I'm joining the army. I'm getting married. There might be a war.

"Let me know what you decide to do?" That was my dad's answer to the idea that war might be coming.

I hung up the phone and went to the volunteer office to find out if I could stay after classes ended. A week later, I moved out of student housing and into my own room in one of the older buildings on the kibbutz. I became a hired worker, like the Germans at that first kibbutz, like the British here at this one. I took whatever job I was assigned to and I tried not to complain. In my free time, I read books and drank beer and listened to the BBC world service on my little shortwave radio.

And I started hanging out with Alastair, a tall, skinny Englishman in his early twenties. One of those unemployed British guys, Alastair was angry at the world, disliked Americans by default, and somehow decided I was interesting enough to give his free time to. Because I had learned nothing, I was flattered.

I turned eighteen that winter. I don't remember my birthday.

CHAPTER NINE:
Lost Boys and Lost Girls

The main characters in *Peter Pan* are Wendy and the Lost Boys. Wendy ends up getting the shitty end of things, taking care of the boys and sewing on Peter Pan's shadow and I don't remember what else. The boys mostly got to play. They were in Neverland not growing up because, I don't know, Margaret Thatcher and Ronald Reagan and unemployment and something about "public school." Public school is confusing to Americans because in the United States, the public schools are the regular people schools. In Britain, they're the private schools where you graduate with a fancy accent like Trevor had. Economic class and capitalism have something to with all this not growing up, too, I guess, though I could never figure out how that worked, exactly.

We had rich kids and not-so-rich kids in my California neighborhood. My high school boyfriend Sam, and Mackey, with her mechanic dad, were not so rich, but I don't think they were poor. They lived in houses—not apartments—and the kids had their own rooms. My dad and my stepmom pretended we were rich. My dad drove a Mercedes. My stepmom shopped at the high-end department stores, never second-hand. We had a nice house on top of a hill. The only reason I knew we weren't rich is because I would overhear them talking about money troubles. I didn't think much about any of this—which is a good sign we were well enough off—before I met these English lost boys—and some girls—who could tell you what class the other guy was by his accent.

Alastair was sort of middle class, or his family was, anyway. He'd gone to a public school—the paid for kind. After graduation, he could not find work because of England's bad job market. His friend Ben was from northern England, from a working-class family. Alastair and Ben weren't friends with Trevor. They hated him for being in Israel by choice, not out of necessity. There was another English girl who was kind of fancy and blonde and claimed to be somehow "in the theater," but I didn't really know her. She was always off with her Israeli boyfriend. When she was around, she just wanted to talk about fucking her Israeli boyfriend, and honestly, it got boring fast. Brian the Texan, the guy Ronnie had been sleeping with, was a lost boy too, different from the English guys but just as lost. He had started drinking like it was his second job. When he wasn't working or eating, he was drinking.

It was like all these people—myself included—were trying to cross into being grown adults, but the road had washed out. The Brits did not want to go back to England because there was no work, but there was no way to go forward, either. Almost everyone around me had something else going on. Hardly anyone was just on vacation. Brian was hiding from, and with, his alcohol problem. Alastair had run away from a bleak economy. Judith was religious, the most religious American Jew I'd ever been friends with, but she was conflicted. She could not figure out how to be a religious Jew and a lesbian at the same time. And it turned out she was not totally a lesbian, either, but bisexual. I'd see her leaving Ben's room in the morning when I was coming out of Alastair's. She had stopped telling me I needed to try it with a woman once she started sleeping with Ben.

If you wanted to be anyone, you wanted to be one of the Swedish girls. They had fewer worries than anyone else. Sweden did not have England or Germany's bad economy. The girls weren't running away from a recession. They weren't Jewish, so they weren't trying to find a connection to the tribe. They weren't Israeli, so if the war got too close, they could leave. It seemed like the Swedish girls just wanted some sun and to fuck Israeli boys. They were the only ones having a really good time.

The Jewish Agency brochures don't really tell you who you're going to meet in their Promised Land indoctrination program. The pictures are all healthy young Jewish faces, Israelis with their tanned olive skin, their work clothes. Fresh faced American kids in clean t-shirts and shorts, posing in groups around tractors. The pictures don't show the lost boys and girls, skinny and sunburned in thread-bare jeans. They don't show the outside workers slogging through physical labor, scraping up change for beer. They don't show this messy accidental collision of people trading books and hooking up and listening to shortwave radio and trying to get along.

Alastair made fun of the California anthem rock I liked, the stuff I listened to in high school, but he loved new wave music and he loved to dance. The radio was always on when we were together. Sometimes, there'd be dance nights in the community lounge. We'd turn the lights down and drink more beer than usual. Alastair was always in the center of it, throwing his long legs and arms around, swirling in the middle of all the music—Madness and Roxy Music and The Police.

He seemed more puzzled by me than anything else. I liked that. Somehow, I'd started bringing my shortwave radio to Alastair's room and we'd stay up late, drinking coffee, gossiping about everyone. I told him about what had happened with Trevor.

"Yes, you are an idiot," he said, "but that guy is a total tool." He went off on a rant about Trevor and his kind being everything wrong with England, what with his fancy education and accent and fuck those people. I didn't understand that Alastair had had the same fancy education he was making fun of. I couldn't tell the difference between how Alastair and Trevor talked, but Alastair sure made a big deal out of it. It was weird, Alastair didn't seem to think I was very smart, and he was always making sharp-edged remarks about Americans, but I convinced myself he was on my side because he hated Trevor. I don't know when I stopped going back to my own room at night, but I did, and then we were together.

When I moved what little stuff I had into Alastair's tiny room, it was exciting, grown up. I was shacking up with my blue-eyed English boyfriend. The next evening, he threw a glass of milk at me while I was sitting on the bed. And then he laughed.

I had come back from the cafeteria with milk for our coffee. It was late in the afternoon. I was sitting on the bed reading. Alastair was making coffee, and when it was done, he threw the milk at me. Just swung his arm, loose, and sent the milk flying everywhere in a long slow white arc, soaking my shirt, my hair. We weren't fighting, we were hanging out like you do when your workday is over, and he just lost it. That's wrong. He didn't lose it, nothing changed before he threw the milk at me. It was almost like he was seeing what would happen if he did something awful to me.

I was deeply confused. I grabbed a clean shirt and went to the washroom. I looked at myself in the mirror, my shirt dripping, milk in my hair. It was ridiculous. I stuck my head under the shower, changed my clothes, and rinsed my shirt out in the sink. I stared in the mirror some more and finally, got the nerve to back to what had been our room for two days. Was it two days?

"Why did you do that?" I asked.

"I don't know," he said. "I just saw you sitting there, and I got so angry."

When nobody's treated you right for a while, you forget what it's supposed to look like. I know it sounds stupid; I know. Obviously, you don't go throwing your drink at someone you care about, and you don't put up with it if you're on the receiving end. You do something else. You do anything else. I should have done something else. I should have taken my things and gone back to my room. I should have asked to go back on whatever shift would keep me away from Alastair. I should have told someone. I should have called home and said, *I've had enough, I need to come home.* But I didn't. None of those things seemed possible.

Also, being treated badly is embarrassing. It feels like you must have done something wrong. It feels like it's somehow your fault, because nothing about it makes any sense. It's unbelievable too—I literally could not believe what had happened. And unlike when Hannes crashed into my bed in the night, no one had seen it. There I was, embarrassed, and I felt like I'd be lying even while I was hanging my shirt to dry on the laundry line out front.

If I was going to tell someone, if I was going to ask for help, it had to be someone I trusted. Someone who would say, "I believe you. Here's the key to my place, go there, and we will figure out how to make you safe."

But Ronnie had gone back to Boston. Brian, the Texan with a drinking problem, had gone to another farm. Something had happened, he had gotten drunk and he'd been found behind the dumpsters, and then he was gone. I did not know Judith well enough to ask for her help. Plus, she was busy not being a lesbian with Ben, two doors over. The American immigrant, the guy I'd worked the factory shifts with probably would have done something if I'd asked. But after Hannes got thrown off the kibbutz for crawling into my bed, I could not bear the idea of being iced out by the British. I couldn't shoulder the scorn they'd heap on me were Alastair to get sent away. If Alastair were sent away, I would have to relive that whole scene.

I went for a walk around the grounds and when I came back, Alastair acted like nothing had happened. I was annoyed and per- plexed, but I thought the only thing hurt was my pride. Maybe it wasn't that big of a deal after all. That's how I decided to act, like it was no big deal.

Here's another thing about being abused—because that what it turned into when Alastair started punching me until my arms and legs were covered with big purple marks. You want to believe it's over when your abuser says it's over. I mean, why would not you want to believe it? I would cry and beg Alastair to stop, stop it, you're hurting me, and he would. He would stop. And then he was so apologetic. He would be sweet; he would beg me to forgive him. And I would, over and over. I would forgive him, and I would believe he was not going to hurt me again. I wanted to believe, every time, that this was the last time. I didn't know that the first time should be the last time. I didn't know that the only way to make it the last time was to be com- pletely out of reach.

It would not be entirely right to say I felt trapped. I had a little bit of money, and I had very good language skills. I was capable of put- ting on my shoes, picking up my bag, and going somewhere else. But I had no idea where to go.

I thought about my high school friend Casey, pregnant and sent away as though she was the one who'd done something wrong. I couldn't go back to Casey's house. Going to Ian's was out of the question. He was going through his own scene, trying to figure out how to be gay and out and his own person. It's not like I could ask him to support me. Mackey had started cosmetology school and that made no sense to me at all. The things she thought were important seemed frivolous to me. I did not know how I would talk to her. She cared about hair and makeup and nail polish and I cared about—I couldn't say what, but not those things. She was still living with her parents too; she didn't have her own place. My mom was getting married, and I was pretty sure the reason I'd been sent to live with my dad was that she couldn't deal with me. And my dad, I had no idea what was going on with my dad. The process servers. The overheard conversations about money. The way he didn't listen when I talked. "Sounds like everything is going great!" It felt like there was no home for me to go.

Maybe Eli's dad was right when he said there was something wrong with me. Why on earth *had* I been sent away? Why hadn't anyone told me to come home? When I called my parents the first time, the second time, to let them know we were being shelled but I was okay, they believed me. I wasn't directly harmed by the artillery rockets, so I guess I was technically okay. But I don't remember anyone saying, "You should come home. Things are weird here, but we'd rather you weren't in an actual war zone. Do you have enough money to buy a plane ticket?" No one asked if I was scared. No one questioned what I was saying. No one said "Hey, are you sure you're okay? Are you sure you don't want to come home? Things are changing here, but we'll figure it out. Come home." It would have been nice to be asked.

It was easier to believe Alastair when he told me he was sorry. It was easier to believe he would not hurt me again than it was to consider alternatives. It was easier to wear long-sleeved shirts, to wear shorts below the knee to hide my bruises. It was easier to dress modestly, what with the Israeli boys trying to pick up any unaccompanied young woman, especially if she looked like she might be American. Believing Alastair and putting up with these passing storms was easier than facing the truth of what was happening—that I was in an abusive relationship. It was easier than figuring out what to do about it. In Israel, you did not know there was a war on until the days when you did, and my life with Alastair was the same.

While it was still dark, the alarm would go off and Alastair and I would get up and go to work. Sometimes weekends we'd go to Jerusalem and wander the old city ignoring the hawkers, buying pastries and plates of hummus and staying in mostly empty hostels. We'd walk the city walls and look across the West Bank toward Jordan. We'd talk about visiting the ancient city of Petra and do nothing to make that trip happen.

Because my Hebrew had advanced so much, I'd do the talking when it came to paying the hostel bill, or bargaining for the black and white kaffiyeh scarves that we wore around our necks. Or getting a locker at the bus station to store our gear so we could sleep on the beach in Tel Aviv. The beach was notorious for petty thieves who would wander the sea wall. They'd ask sleeping backpackers for matches to see if you were awake. There was no risk of physical harm, but if you thought your wallet was safe because you were sleeping on top of it, you were wrong. Alastair and I had the same kind of adventures I'd had with Eli, though now I was the social one because I had the language. And sometimes, at night, Alastair would hit me until I begged him to stop. Then he would promise not to do it again and I would believe him.

Alastair and I ran the clock down on our contracts and then signed up for another posting in the south, near the Gaza border. The Gaza Strip was a Palestinian region occupied by the Israelis, a stronghold for Palestinian separatists. The kibbutz, just two miles from the Gaza border, lived with the memory of the 1948 Arab–Israeli war as though it were yesterday. There were life sized cutouts of soldiers placed in the fields, just outside the residential area, to remind you how close Egyptians soldiers had come to the kibbutz. The land was politically charged, but to us it was just an Arab region with a beach, a place you could put your feet in the water once you crossed the army checkpoint.

In this new place, Alastair was angry all the time. It got worse when the kibbutz program director took our room away. They had too many workers and they didn't care that we were a couple. I moved into a triple room next door, and an American guy moved in with Alastair. Alastair barricaded himself behind a wardrobe against the back wall of the room, and I bunked with a Scottish girl and an English girl whom I could not be bothered to make friends with. I felt defeated by the change. Alastair was the only familiar thing and though he wasn't safe, he was consistent. He would have to do.

I'd renewed my visa once, twice, and on the last time, the agent, dressed in full military uniform, told me that he would not renew it again. It was strange that he didn't tell me it was time to make *Aliyah*, to become an Israeli citizen. I was strong, young, Jewish, unmarried, and street-fluent in the local language. Shouldn't he be telling me to get serious and stay? The officer stamped my passport, wham, wham, and looked at me.

"This is the last time I'll renew your visa. You've been in country too long."

The Israelis didn't want me either.

Maybe it wasn't the officer's job to tell me to emigrate; maybe the next move was all mine. I didn't want to become an Israeli, though. Israel had given me a whole new language, but she had provided nothing but uncertainties. The aggressions of her sons, who acted like I was their toy. Military attacks from the outside. The abuses of her guests, who she tolerated because hey, cheap labor keeps the crops coming in. In exchange for all of this, you never had to explain to anyone about being Jewish. Not a fair deal. I decided it was time to give up. I counted my money and found I had enough to go home. I called my dad and booked a flight back to California. It couldn't be worse than this.

My final day on the kibbutz, Alastair and I walked out to the highway. I stood on the two-lane blacktop to hitch a ride to the beach in Gaza one last time. Alastair hung back so the drivers couldn't see him before they stopped. We walked out onto the sand barefoot, tar stuck to our feet. There were oil tankers offshore, and a few Palestinian boys throwing a ball on the beach, their moms watching from a distance. We walked in the water and did not talk.

CHAPTER TEN:
You Can't Go Home Again

Alastair and I went to Tel Aviv and spent one night sleeping in the hedges behind an apartment building because he did not feel like paying for a hostel. We wandered a residential neighborhood near the bus station until we found a place with a back garden. We unrolled our sleeping bags between the bushes and the building's ground floor windows. Alastair spent the night alternating between punching me and swatting away mosquitoes. The following night, we slept on the floor at the airport. My flight was very early the next day. I was dirty and sweaty from forty-eight hours of living rough in the heat, my shoulders sore from bruises. I was exhausted, completely exhausted.

We said a blurry goodbye, and as I headed to security, I started to cry. I had to enter a closet-sized space where a guard told me to place my day pack on a folding table. I tried pay attention to this serious young woman in full uniform, a pistol strapped to her waist.

"Where are you going? How long have you been in Israel? What were you doing here? Where do you live?" She flipped through my passport and unzipped my day pack, placing my camera and my Walkman on the table between us. "Where did you get these?"

I answered her questions as best I could, breathing deep between words. "I've been a volunteer; I'm going home to California. I got my camera there, it was a gift, and the Walkman too." But I could not stop crying. She paused and looked at me.

"Why are you crying?" she asked, with the same distant, professional tone she'd used for all her questions. I told her I had just parted ways with my boyfriend. She eyed me, peered one last time into my beat-up backpack, and let me enter the departures terminal.

I cried at the gate while waiting to board my flight, and I cried when I wedged into my window seat on the plane. I cried until I fell asleep and when I woke up, the people who had been seated next to me were gone. I started crying again. I don't know if they moved because I was crying, but it could well have been because I smelled like two days on the streets of Tel Aviv. I cried some more while waiting for my connecting flight in New York and then, I cried all the way across the United States. I was still crying when I saw my dad at the gate. I cried a when I saw my stepmom, who told me I looked healthy, but asked what sewer I had been sleeping in. "It was a hedge one night, and the airport the next," I corrected. I cried until I arrived at the baggage claim and saw my friend Ian, who had come with my family to meet me. He hugged me hard and told me how much he'd missed me. His smile was so big and so real that I finally stopped crying.

I spent the first few days in a haze. I was jetlagged and confused and completely wrung out. My dad and my stepmom were indulgent. They let me sleep. They put a place at the table for me and left me alone, mostly. I doted on my baby brother. I was happy to babysit him while my dad and stepmom did whatever they were doing at the time. My brother was content in my company. I would read to him and sit him in my lap. I'd put him in his crib when it was naptime, and then

I'd go sit in the back yard in the sunshine and do nothing for a while. I'd come back in the house to hear him screaming at the top of his lungs, not because he needed anything, but because he was discovering that he had his own voice. I'd peek in his room to ask him what he was doing, and he'd light up and giggle at me. He was such good medicine, this joyful little boy. He wanted nothing from me, he had no questions, and he just liked it when I was around.

There was no way I could stay, though. I could tell things weren't right. I'd overhear the same conversations about money over and over, how much they were struggling. My dad was talking about selling the house. Something was up. To complicate things, my stepmom and I simply did not like each other. This wasn't new. Not long after my brother had been born, while I was still in high school, she'd confronted me. We'd been at odds about something. I don't remember what it was. She was standing on the stairs, wrapped in a towel. Maybe she'd had a good think while she was in there because it seemed like she'd come directly from the shower to confront me.

"Do you want me to take my baby and leave?" she asked me.

I found the whole thing a weird power play. I'd been shuffled off to my dad's house after Casey's parents decided they'd had enough of my supposed bad influence. I wasn't feeling particularly in control.

"You're the adult," I said. "That seems like your decision."

The peace of my homecoming was temporary. I was aware of that. Living with my dad and my stepmom would not help me find my way to whatever was next. I had a roof over my head, I was safe, there were no bombs; that was good. There was no boyfriend with a temper that could strike—not like lightning, because you could see that coming, you could see the sky change, you believed it was real. Alastair's temper was something else: sudden, sharp, and then gone as if you'd imagined it. But the house was, well, it was not home for me. It was a fueling station, a recovery ward. It was a picnic table at a roadside turnout. A place to unfold the map and figure out where I was supposed to go next.

My dad wanted us all to get along. There was a mysterious lawsuit, money problems, the house needed to be sold at a loss. He had other things to think about. My stepmom was wrapped up in all of that, plus, she was devoted to her son. She did not need me, a confused young woman trying to launch her own life, muddying the waters.

Nothing about our daily lives made sense to me. I felt I was missing some key piece of information. We had a housekeeper and my stepmom would go shopping at the mall, in the expensive stores, Saks Fifth Avenue and I. Magnin. But money was tight and if I ate the wrong thing from the hall pantry I got in trouble. We couldn't just go eating artichoke hearts for a snack; do you know how much those cost? I did not know how much they cost, no. Was it more than the shoes she brought home today, the blouse she brought home yesterday, the kitchenware that there already seemed to be more than enough of? Did we have money or didn't we? If we were in such trouble, why was there a housekeeper? Why was there so much shopping? My dad had a Mercedes station wagon. We didn't seem to be living like people who had financial problems.

I reconnected with Ian and Mackey. Ian and I roamed around directionless; Mackey was building her career. She had a contract with a salon and was painting nails for a living. She enjoyed it so much I had a hard time making fun of her, even though it didn't make any sense to me. Ian was sleeping on someone's couch somewhere. We were spiraling off in different directions, but Mackey had started to find her place in the world. She was living like what a real adult was supposed to live like, while Ian and I, we were still searching. Mackey had a boyfriend who was tall and athletic had gold highlights in his hair. He was attractive and knew it, but I didn't like him. He only wanted to talk about his own looks. Mackey seemed so happy, though, so I kept my mouth shut about him. I did not want what she had, but I was still jealous. I was jealous that she seemed to know what she wanted, that she knew how to get it.

I'd been home for two weeks when Alastair's letters started to arrive. He'd gone back to England not long after I'd left Israel. He had stopped going to his kibbutz work shifts and repeatedly went to Gaza to walk on the beach, he wrote. After blowing off work one time too many, the volunteer coordinator told him he had to leave. He had somehow got back to England and moved to a studio apartment in a rough neighborhood in London. He worked at a garage a few blocks away. He sent me British music magazines, which I devoured. I asked Mackey to drive me to record stores where I could buy the stuff that was hot in the British press. He told me how much he ached for me. The longing would pour out of the thin blue envelopes in the kind of language a girl who is eighteen could only dream about. I couldn't believe he was the same guy who was so angry, so mean. In the confusion of my half-baked California existence I reinvented Alastair as someone who was just angry sometimes. He was someone who wanted me, that's all I could remember, all I could hear when I read his letters.

Maybe I should have been thinking about applying to community college, about taking some classes, but I was so unfocused. I got a job at the mall. The store was the kind of place that sold cheap fashion to people who cared what they looked like but didn't have a lot of money. To work the sales floor, you had to be fashionable. To work the downstairs stock room, like I did, you had to like being alone. I read books and tagged merchandise and clocked in and out. I'm pretty sure the upstairs staff forgot I was there most days.

The manager asked me if I wanted to advance to the sales floor, like that was a good thing, a promotion. But I had to take a lie detector test to do that job, and I was going to need better clothes. The salesgirls got paid commission, which I thought meant you had to tell strangers they looked great so they would spend more money. I did not have anything against cheap clothes. I just did not want to lie to strangers. Plus, one of the other shop girls had burst into tears during her lie detector test. It was mean and distrustful. Like a machine could show you the truth about someone's character, what the hell was that? I lied preemptively and told them my dad did not want me taking the test. This was a bad excuse, especially because I was of legal age to make my own choices. But refusing the test allowed me to stay in the stock room, where I could read Alastair's letters over and over. Sometimes I pried the security tags off the few items of clothing I wanted to prove I could steal. The mere existence of that lie detector test made me want to steal things just to make a point.

Ian would show up at the store during my break and we'd go get lunch in the food court. I'd tell him about my time in Israel and he'd listen, not saying anything about his own life. I did not ask. I was so completely wrapped up in everything I was leaving out. I wanted someone to listen so I could make space in my head for the things I did not want anyone to know.

I took the bus to work, I took the bus home. Sometimes, Ian picked me up, or Mackey, if she was not working. And sometimes, one or both of them would stay for dinner with my family. Ian and Mackey were always welcome. My stepmom liked them both, and my dad did too. My stepmom and Mackey both cared about fashion, so they had that in common. Ian was always polite and kind, so of course my parents liked him. They treated him like he was my boyfriend, but Ian was still gay and still not telling anyone. I did not feel the need to correct that misunderstanding, mostly because I didn't know what it meant. We were friends, I trusted him; that was all I needed to know. The three of us watched TV and listened to records. We had mostly given up getting high because I did not want to pay for weed and Mackey always had to work. I was saving every dime I earned to buy a ticket to London where, in a clearly stupid act of amnesia, I had planned to rejoin Alastair.

I missed him. Yes, he could be unspeakably mean, but his temper was a fire engine going past with the siren on. The quiet came back and it was over. You could hear the kids playing in the street again, and the birds singing, and all my bruises were gone. This was what I told myself, anyway, that every time it was temporary, and once it passed, it was better than anything else I had going on. I'd forgotten that he hurt me, over and over.

There was something else driving me to leave home again, though. I had picked up this fever, an addict's craving for somewhere else. The high of being in strange cities, of being surrounded by languages not my own, the buzz I got when from navigating myself to the right place through a system I did not understand—it was always thrilling. I wanted to feel that way all the time. My feelings about Alastair had become so tangled up with my feelings about travel. I could not tell them apart. It seemed like the only way to get that sense of adventure back was to find my way back to Alastair and see where it would take me.

Three months in, I quit my job at the mall. I bought a ticket to London, packed a bag, and left California behind. Again.

CHAPTER ELEVEN:
Electric Avenue

Alastair lived in a studio walk-up apartment with a queen-sized bed in the middle of the room. There was a two-burner cooker on a shelf, a half-sized fridge, and a café-sized Formica-topped table. A bay window with a bench seat overlooked a street full of red brick three-story row house apartments, all of them the same. The heat came from an electric fireplace just opposite the foot of the bed. The toilet was in a little closet on the landing, just outside the door, and on the next landing down, there was a cold, dimly lit room with a big claw foot bathtub. Everything was powered by one-pound coin-fed meters, including the hot water for the bath. Because the bathroom was unheated, it was easy to spend the first pound running enough hot water to warm up the cast iron tub.

Alastair worked as an assistant mechanic in an auto shop just around the corner from his apartment. He got up early every morning, slurped a cup of tea and headed off to work. After he left, I'd huddle in front of the red glow from the electric heater and read books, old Penguin classics: Orwell's *Down and Out in London and Paris*, Dickens' *Great Expectations*, Austen's *Pride and Prejudice*. Alastair had stacks of them, and I had somehow made it out of high school without reading these works, save for *Les Miserable's* in French. I read it again in English and wondered why I hadn't cheated in class? I could have read the book in English then written my paper in French. Instead, I slogged through the original Hugo like there was no other way to accomplish this task. I didn't have to fail French, but I wasn't very imaginative about passing it, either.

If the weather was good—and sometimes even when it was not—I would walk to Brixton Station to catch the tube and go visit a museum. I went to the British Museum to see the Rosetta stone and those marbles that were stolen from Greece. I walked through endless hallways of furniture at the Victoria and Albert. I visited the transit museum with its vintage trolley cars and the portrait gallery and Westminster Abbey. I ducked into churches to try to get warm from the damp London winter. It was like I was on an unstructured survey course on the history of Western Culture.

And London, how I loved the rough city living of Brixton compared to the neat life of the California suburbs. I wandered the Electric Avenue market, past fishmongers and produce sellers, often completely overwhelmed by Cockney and Caribbean accents. I walked away from conversations more than once because I could not understand what the shopkeepers were saying. London was predictably gray and cold. I did not have the right clothes for it so I would bundle up as best I could knowing that it would just be a few blocks to the station, where I'd be inside again. It was always just a few blocks to a museum entrance. If the cold got to be too much, I'd duck into a café, order a cup of strong milky tea, and sit in a window, wiping the condensation off with my sleeve so I could watch the people go by outside. I never learned to like tea with milk. It was too rich for my taste and the flavor of the milk always left a weird feeling on my tongue. But that's how it came when I ordered it, and it made me warm inside.

If the weather was especially bad, I would put on Alastair's big wool sweater, drink endless cups of weak black tea with honey, and read like I was starving for words. Sometimes I would buy a Sunday *Guardian* and take all week to read every single page. Alastair would come home, scrub the shop dirt off his hands, and we would eat baked beans on toast for dinner and listen to BBC 4. The seventies rock I'd grown up didn't get airplay here, but there was no shortage of great dance music. Alastair turned it up when the Commodores came on, or Earth, Wind & Fire. I loved all the new wave bands, everyone in eyeliner, the boys and the girls, Duran Duran and Ultra Vox and ABC. We did not have a TV, but I didn't miss it because there was always something on the radio. There was always new music to sing along with. And the BBC had sprawling soap opera serials, and dramatic theater plays, big round accents performing Shakespeare or George Bernard Shaw or Agatha Christie or P. G. Wodehouse. I was endlessly entertained.

Alastair was even tempered and sweet. On the weekends we'd go have a round or two at the pub on the corner. I was still too young to drink legally in California, but in London, it was fine. The first time I had a Guinness I could barely walk away from it. I was full as though I'd had a complete meal and more than a little bit drunk. We ordered black and tans like they were some kind of layered dessert, the dark Guinness floating on top of whatever pale ale the pub was pouring. Sometimes we'd get fish and chips wrapped in newspaper and sit in the too-bright shops shaking malt vinegar on everything for the sharp flavor. We'd go out for big English breakfasts in dumpy little cafés— though like tea with milk, I never learned to prefer an English breakfast over an American one. They were always too greasy, too meaty for my tastes. The cheap places Alastair chose were never as good as what we could make at home, but it felt indulgent to Alastair to eat breakfast out, so we did.

Some nights, we'd meet Alastair's friends to shoot pool and drink beer. We went to a party in a dark house that was full of loud music and people smoking. We made out on the stairs and went home to bed. Mostly Alastair went to work, and I read books and that was all there was. It was a good life but it's not like either one of us wanted it to continue like this forever. I could not work—I didn't have a work permit—and I did not want Alastair supporting me. There was no clear path to education here, either. My brain was good enough but enrolling in college seemed as easy as going to the moon.

We talked about getting married so we could go back to the United States together. There was better work in the States, at least, and if we were married, he'd be able to get a work permit. It never occurred to me to think about what kind of work that would be, or how much it would cost us to get a place of our own back in California. Still, we pretended this was an idea worth looking into. There was no romance in it, none at all; it was another option on a menu of things that would help us figure how to have adult lives.

I took the Tube to the embassy where I asked the receptionist at the desk, a towering Englishman in full uniform, what it would take to get a visa for my fiancé. How quickly that could happen? "Excuse me, miss," he said, "This would not be a marriage of convenience, would it?" He was so polite that I did not laugh. I did not respond that actually, no, it was very inconvenient at best. I left with a stack of paperwork, forms and requirements, which Alastair and I reviewed that night.

"I have to prove I can be financially responsible for you," I told him, "That's not going to happen. Plus, this is going to take months." We threw out the idea and the paperwork. Not for a second would I have considered asking my parents to sign for Alastair's immigration. We gave up on the idea of going back to the United States together almost as quickly as we'd come upon it. Not getting married, not going to America. Next.

We decided instead to blow our savings on travel. Cut loose from the framework of everyday life we would skid across the surface of the globe and end up in India where we would, well, we would figure that out when we got there. One day, we borrowed a car and drove north to ditch Alastair's stacks of books and his other belongings at his parents' house. Alastair had grown up in a suburb of sturdy brick houses where the gardens were neat and had low fences out in front. I understood why Alastair had fled for Israel: the sameness was depressing.

While we were in his hometown, Alastair took me to the places he'd hung out as a boy. Down to the river, under an iron bridge, to playgrounds, and once we went to have tea at a garden center. At night, he slept in his old room and I slept in his sister's bed two doors down the hall. "I told my mother you sleep on the couch," Alastair said, implying chastity in both of us that I'm sure she did not believe.

She looked so much like him, the same unruly hair, the same deep-set large blue eyes, I found it uncanny. I pictured the hard little sofa in front of the electric fire, how our bed was the biggest thing in the room. I imagined myself lying sleepless on the scratchy upholstery while Alastair sprawled across the queen-sized bed. If Alastair's mom had ever come to visit, she would have known he was lying. I'm sure she knew he was lying without seeing the apartment.

Alastair's father was a dentist, serious and conservative, with hopes that Alastair would become a real estate agent. According to his dad, Alastair had thrown away his chances when he'd been arrested for stealing a case of wine from the market where he'd been working his first year out of school. This petty crime, which I saw as a careless indiscretion, not an indication of a permanent criminal nature, created a rift between Alastair and his father that could only be repaired by Alastair's buckling down and getting a real estate license.

Alastair's short career as a thief was uninteresting. It was easy for me to imagine the bunch of brash young guys on the loading dock deciding that one missing box would be noticed by no one. But Alastair's father had been angry with him since the day he had to bail him out. Angry since he had to go with Alastair to court. I only wanted to know if the judges wore those wigs and robes like I'd seen in British comedies on public television. They did.

Despite his father's plans, Alastair had no intention of doing something as pedestrian as showing apartments to prospective buyers. That's part of why he had gone to Israel in the first place. His father would have paid for the training, but Alastair was not interested. Living on unemployment for so long in a bad market had become depressing, so he'd joined the tide of wanderers who'd ended up doing kibbutz work.

The economy had improved some after he went back to England. But he had that same restlessness that had infected me, that itching desire to be somewhere else. There was not going to be any buckling down to do anything, anything at all. His dad seemed to think relentless badgering would make Alastair come to his senses about this very specific future, but anyone outside the situation could see there was no way that was ever going to happen.

Alastair owned a suit, an expensive pinstripe number. I'd made him dress in it once so I could see what he'd look like, cleaned up and grown up. I knew him as dirty from the fields or covered in shop grease from the garage. On his best-dressed days, he'd be in a beat-up wool sweater and a pair of jeans. He was so disdainful of anything that held the tiniest whiff of establishment. The suit didn't change the expression of ironic superiority he wore on his face. It was impossible to picture him unlocking the front door on a neat little house and asking a young couple what they thought of the kitchen. Wouldn't that dormered upstairs bedroom be cute for their little girl? No way. "Bunch of fucking wankers," he'd have said, and walked away in his long-legged stride, flipping them off as he went. A real estate agent. What a joke.

We chose to travel instead. We would figure it out as we went along. We would find work and bounce across the map, and it would be okay. Alastair gave up the dreary London apartment and quit his job at the mechanic. We headed east with a very general itinerary—Paris, Athens, places east of there—and not much else.

CHAPTER TWELVE:
Let's Go

My bag held my dog-eared *Let's Go Europe*, a one set of long underwear, a second pair of jeans. A few ragged t-shirts, a wrap skirt. I strapped a sleeping bag to the lash points on the bottom of my pack, and I carried my camera, the fat strap wrapped around my wrist. I had another little bag I wore around my neck that held my passport, my traveler's checks, and whatever cash I had on me. Alastair had the same absurdly minimal amount of gear, but what did we need, anyway?

We had hitchhiked to Dover where we walked onto the ferry and off into our unplanned journey. Our minimalist plan was to spend a few days in Paris and then, continue south to Greece, unless a better idea surfaced. Alastair had heard there was work in Greece, but what kind and how we would find it, he did not specify. Maybe it was farm work. Restaurant work. Resort work. No matter. This nonspecific work was out there. It would find us, and we would sustain ourselves on it.

I believed this myth about work because I wanted it to be true. Once our pockets were lined with the Greek *drachmas* we'd earn doing who knows what, we would wind our way to India, overland as much as possible. Our lives would be a dashed line on the map, like a transitional scene in an old movie. A propeller plane flies intrepid explorers across inky mountains. A compass rose decorates one corner of the page; sea monsters carve holes through oceans of hand drawn waves. We would travel overland through Iran and Afghanistan.

We didn't know what we were doing or where, exactly, we were going. We were completely unprepared, and this worried us not at all. We never asked ourselves why India was our goal or what we would do when we got there. It was not important to know. The thing was to be in motion, to hurl ourselves like skipping stones across the planet for as far and with as many rippling jumps as possible.

When I signed up for junior high school French, it wasn't because I was so keen on learning languages. It was about art. I grew up in a house full of art. When my parents were still married, they collected art and I loved our trips to the galleries in San Francisco. I also loved the heavy picture books on our shelves, the full color plates of the ceiling in the Sistine Chapel, the photos of Picasso in his studio. I loved my art classes; they were the one thing I never skipped in high school. I loved being inside my head and making something out of nothing but color and shape. I could draw, I could see color. Art was something I felt an inherent understanding for, so different than math, which I struggled through. I dreamed of the day I would visit the Louvre to see the *Mona Lisa* and her coy smile. The day I could visit Seurat's *Saturday in the Park* to see all those little dots in person. This is why I studied French; it was the language of artists.

During my junior year of high school, my dad and stepmom told me they'd send me to Paris to study art after graduation. It would have pleased them to send me off to Paris to study art, probably the same way it pleased them to send me to Israel to be with the tribe. It was like them to make crazy promises with no real information about what was required. Their promise that I'd go study art in Paris didn't matter anymore; I had got myself to Paris by other means. I could not have been more delighted.

Alastair and I found an attic room with a sink and a bidet. The shower and the toilet were on the landing in the hall. Our window swung outwards and looked down five or six stories into a narrow cobbled street. At street level, right across from the door to our little hotel there was a tiny market. They had fresh baguettes every morning, a small array of produce. A stout cashier tucked into a corner would reach back to grab cigarettes or envelopes of loose tobacco. We lived on bread and olives and cheese bought from open-air markets, or sometimes omelet sandwiches from little carts along the Seine or in the public gardens.

I dragged Alastair from museum to museum, in and out of churches, up the steps to Sacre Couer and down under the Beaux Arts style subway entrances. He was terrified of heights, but up we went up to stand next to the gargoyles at Notre Dame. We climbed the winding staircase to look down on the Isle de Paris. As I leaned out over the balustrade to touch the monsters on the beak, Alastair backed into the stairwell, white with fear. We spent hours in the museums, hours cadging the student discount with the cards we'd acquired from cheap travel shops in London. I swooned over the Degas sculptures, his young ballerina paintings made three dimensional in bronze. Swooned over the giant Renaissance masterworks in the Louvre, the immaculately laid out gardens around the city. I snapped photos of the paintings I loved as though the act of taking a picture would help me own them. I snapped pictures of the statues on the steps of the opera. And I snapped pictures of Alastair in front of our window in our room which was an actual rooftop garret, like a place an artist in a movie would live.

We splurged on frothy café au laits, served to us while we perched on wrought iron chairs under striped awnings. Once, only once, we went out for dinner and had fist-sized game hens and green beans slathered in butter. My high school French was good enough that I could use it to get around, to buy groceries, to ask for directions, and I was unafraid of making mistakes. The French were kind to me maybe because I tried, and maybe because I was so young. Everything about Paris was exactly as you dream Paris to be when you are a girl who studies French and wants to go to art school. I was eighteen and in Paris with my English boyfriend. I was a character in a novel of my own invention, and it was easy to erase the parts I did not want to see, to instead experience Paris exactly as I had imagined it would be. Better, maybe.

We watched our money dwindle, even while we tried not to spend much of it. But we had to eat, and we needed a place to sleep, and we were in Paris, an expensive big city. Our time there was just a deep breath before the hard travel was to begin, a vacation after Alastair's job in the mechanic shop, after the grind and gray of a dreary London winter. A week passed, and then we decided to move on.

We bought long-haul bus tickets to Brindisi, in Italy. There, we would board a ferry to Greece where we would find this work Alastair insisted was out there. It wouldn't be great money, but we'd be paid in cash, and we'd live, well—we'd figure that out once we got there. The cost of living would be cheap, and the weather would be good, and sure, it would all work out somehow.

The bus rolled across France into northern Italy, while miles of road spooled out underneath us. We dozed and stared out the window. Sometimes the bus stopped for a break and we stumbled into brown roadside cafes to eat brown roadside café food.

Once I awoke from a deep sleep and looked out the window at a funeral procession. On a muddy hillside, a dozen or so bent over people carried a coffin. It was raining, everyone was dressed in black, and they all looked so old. I felt a terrible longing to get off the bus right there, to stand in the rain with those grieving people and find out who they were. So many things were happening outside as we slashed through Europe, heading east and south through a front of bad weather. The landscape looked like of the color had been sucked out of it, everything concrete gray and dark brown, I wondered what the food would be like—terrible, I imagined—and how we would communicate—not at all. It's not like it was all attractive romantic scenery. Still, I was hit hard with this desire to be out in it, to be moving much more slowly, to take a moment to sit inside the tiny church at the top of the brown hill. I wanted to see everything I was missing as more than a rainy smear in the distance. And then it was gone, the funeral was gone, all the people were gone, just a reflection on the streaky glass window.

We traveled the full length of Italy's boot overnight, waking to use the bathrooms in small town bus stations that smelled like pee and fried food and cigarettes. Dawn came, and the bus poured us out at the port in Brindisi. We did not see Italy at all; it was no more than a dark blur. I still felt like we had accomplished something merely by covering the distance. I imagined the road miles accruing to me like I was being tattooed with maps of where I'd been.

It did not matter so much where I was; the important thing was where I was not. I was not at my dad's house, a nuisance to be managed in the financial and legal chaos of life there. I was not in college, a goal that was important to me but somehow too abstract to act upon, too inaccessible. I was not in California, shiftless and bored. I had momentum. I was swept up in the idea of motion for its own sake. So long as I kept moving, it did not matter where I was or what I was doing.

At Brindisi, we wandered for a few hours, buying supplies for the ferry ride, drinking tiny cups of gritty, sweet black coffee, reading the English-language newspapers in the racks outside the tobacco shops. The ferry trip to Patras, Greece, was an overnight sailing, departing late in the afternoon. We had passenger tickets only, no cabin, so when we boarded, we headed up on deck and rolled out our sleeping bags with the other backpackers. The weather was on our side. The night was mild and the seas were calm. We chatted with our fellow travelers and dozed until daylight when the ship arrived in Patras on the Peloponnese peninsula.

All of our information came either from fellow travelers or the fat guidebook I carried. Where to stay, where to eat, what to wear, even. There was a steady trickle of backpackers on this same route using some version of the same sources, and we shared what we learned on the road. The same disaffected crew of Germans and British and sometimes Australian wanderers that I'd met on the kibbutz were following the same ant trails across Europe. On the ferry from Brindisi to Patras, rumors said there was work on the island of Corfu, so that's where we headed once we landed. We hitchhiked north.

Hitchhiking in Greece was easy. Truck drivers were willing to stop; maybe they wanted the company. We could not communicate much. The drivers invariably never spoke English—or Spanish or

French or Hebrew—so we would give up after exhausting our limited shared vocabulary. I liked riding in the high truck cabs, peering over the road, watching the countryside roll by. The drivers had decorated their rigs with fringe and religious icons, the cabs had a bunk in the back where we threw our packs. When we had burned out our efforts to talk, the drivers, men with ink black hair and strong arms, would turn up the music and the cab would fill with the sounds of the bouzouki. It was always too loud, but I liked that it was playing. Greece was scrubby low hills and stone farmhouses and sometimes, a ruin, an aqueduct, a few pillars of an ancient temple, would appear on a rise and then drop out of sight as we rolled north.

Corfu was a short ferry ride from the mainland. Parts of this Greek island were outposts for British tourists on holiday. Working-class Brits would stay in small hotels, bake themselves pink in the island's reliable sunshine, and drink ouzo at sidewalk cafés while the sun was setting. The main town—also called Corfu—was all white stucco and little shops selling painted ceramics, peasant dresses, flowered shawls, and strappy leather sandals. It was kitschy and appealing, especially in the late afternoon when everyone seemed to be napping and the cobbled streets were quiet. Alastair wanted nothing to do with it, but I secretly loved how bright and neat everything was. It looked exactly like a postcard of Greece. The buildings were piles of white painted blocks with shocking blue shutters flanking the windows. Old men argued at sidewalk tables and the Ionian Sea was a beautiful turquoise expanse offshore.

But we were not to stay in town. On the ferry, we'd met some English guys who told us about a construction site up the island where Alastair could get work—and maybe I could find something waiting tables. We were eager to pick up some cash. We had blown so much money in Paris and getting to Greece.

The village where the English guys worked was just like Corfu but smaller—pretty, touristy, quiet, with a gorgeous stretch of white sandy beach. We followed the English guys to the concrete shell of someone's unfinished beach house. The guys had set up a squatter's camp in this skeleton of a house; we claimed a corner on the second floor. The place had no windows, no doors; it was just a roof over our heads to keep the rain—or sun—off. Someone had laid a foundation, put up the minimum structure, and given up. I guess there are a lot of different ways to run out of money. I imagined what had happened to these people. Did they have a home life somewhere in England? Had they underestimated what building this place would cost them? Maybe it was a contentious divorce, this place on Corfu the last straw. It was impossible to know.

Alastair joined the English guys' crew, building more of the same kind of places where we made our unofficial camp. Concrete foundations and frames, but better funded than whatever happened with our absentee landowners. He spent eight to ten hours a day mixing and hauling cement. It was brutal physical work for not very much money. He'd start around daybreak and return in the late afternoon, sun baked, his hands blistered, his face spattered with flecks of concrete. While he was working, I went door to door through the restaurants in the village asking if anyone needed English-speaking help. When that failed, I hitchhiked to neighboring towns to do more of the same. I gave up after two weeks and went back to doing the same thing I was doing in London, reading, only this time, it was either on the beach or in our shell of a house. I had picked up Kerouac's *On the Road*, V. S. Naipaul's *Among the Believers*, and a beat-up hardback of *The Great Railway Bazaar*, Paul Theroux's book about traveling in India.

These guys—the writers were all men—wrote about moving through the world. Just like the punk Germans I'd met at my first kibbutz, I wanted to be these men. Untethered to the limitations of daily life, they skittered across the surface of the planet with no regard for time zones and borders. I wanted to be Theroux, especially, looking out the window of the train at a country I did not understand. I'd sit on my sleeping bag, back propped up against the raw concrete of the house and read until Alastair came home from work in the late afternoon. Then we'd go to down to the beach where he'd wash off the day's work in the public showers. We'd watch the sky turn dark while everyone disappeared from the sand until there was no one left but us.

There was a Roma camp just up the road from us. It was a tumble of a place, trailers and little camper vans and the occasional tent, stuck in a patch of trees between the main road and the beach. It was quiet during the day, at night there were campfires and sometimes music from car stereos. They must have seen us coming and going. They had a terrible reputation as thieves, but our stuff, what little stuff we had with us, never went anywhere. I didn't think the Roma were that different than we were, staking a claim on a bit of land not their own, but not being used by anyone else, either.

Two quiet young men from the Roma camp would come over to smoke cigarettes with us. They had olive skin and dark hair. They looked at me like they knew me, like I was their family. They started showing up with sandwiches, just plain white bread sandwiches with some kind of deli meat, but it was welcome.

Alastair was ruthless about spending as little money as possible and when we bought olives and bread and cheese at the village market, he would shoplift chocolate and packages of cookies while I was paying at the register. He never told me about it until we got back from the shop. I hated it, every time he stole something, I was angry with him. I did not want him to get caught. I did not want to be the one to call his parents if something went wrong. What would I do if he ended up handcuffed by some small-town policeman and got locked away? I hated that he was taking advantage of these small shopkeepers. When I told him this, he responded with some nonsense about the evils of capitalism, how they were ripping off the tourists anyway. He was good at shoplifting, and he kept doing it. I was hot with shame every time I learned he had used me as a cover. And I kept eating the chocolate.

The Roma guys came by one day while I was reading in the house alone. They were always so quiet, I never knew they were there until they said *hello*. They squatted on the bare concrete and looked at me. One of them offered me a cigarette. I shook my head. Then the other one looked at me and signed with his hands; it was clear he was asking for sex. I heard my heart beating, I wondered if they could hear it too. The surf crashed in the distance then, everything stopped for a minute. I wondered if I was should be afraid. The sound returned, the sea, kids playing on the sand, the hum of insects in the trees behind the house. I blushed and shook my head again. No. They looked at me, quietly talking to each other in a language I could not understand. Then they got up and left, but not before handing me a stack of sandwiches.

When it was over, I was more flustered by how innocuous the interaction was than anything else. They did not threaten; their body language was free from menace. They had none of the outrage I'd seen men engage in when I'd said *no* in the past. Young Israelis would turn sarcastic and insulting if you declined their advances, like there was something wrong with you. These guys, they asked politely, and when I said no, they took my answer at face value and left.

That day when Alastair returned from work, I told him about the Roma and their proposal. He looked at his shredded palms, raw and cracked from such hard labor, and decided it was time to admit we were beaten. We were running through our funds; it made no sense for us to stay. He went to town to call his father and asked for money to help us move on.

CHAPTER THIRTEEN:

Washed Up

I don't know what Alastair told his father we were going to do with the money. I imagine they argued. I could picture his father telling him to come home, you're not getting any younger, son, I'm not going to make this offer forever. Alastair saying it wasn't going to happen. Maybe Alastair lied, telling his father what he wanted to hear. Alastair was mean and a petty thief. He could have been a liar too. His father wired a few hundred pounds, enough to give us time to decide what to do next, enough to get us both back to England if we went on the cheap like we'd gone on the way down.

We headed the exact opposite direction: southeast, towards Athens.

I was as excited about Athens as I'd been about Paris. In school I'd learned about Greece as the birthplace of Western democracy. I knew the names of Greek philosophers: Socrates and Plato and Aristotle. I imagined the Forum as crowded plaza where you could get coffee and discuss the meaning of existence with strangers. I wanted to see the columns of the Acropolis against the Greek sky, to see where the marbles I'd seen in the British Museum had come from. I was eager to visit another great European city; one important in art and history, a city a people would look at you with interest when you said you'd been there.

It mattered to me what people would think when I'd said I'd been to Athens. More specifically, what they'd say when I told them I'd hitchhiked to Athens. I wanted people to feel impressed with my travels. The truth was not so impressive: I had been a tourist of the worst kind, taking advantage of the people of Corfu while remaining completely ignorant of the culture of the place. We were camping illegally; my boyfriend was shoplifting and working without a permit. I let the island's poorest residents feed me. It didn't occur to me I was taking things away from them too. And it's not like we got out of it ourselves. Alastair's father freed us from our open-air dead-end. I didn't think about any of this. I just wanted to feel tough, worldly, like I could manage on my own anywhere. But I was just another cheap backpacker, barely contributing to the local economy. The tourists Alastair liked to make fun of were better guests than we were.

When the wire transfer from Alastair's father came through, we took the ferry back to the mainland. I wrote ATHINA on a piece of scrap cardboard in big block letters. We walked to the highway. We'd sit on our packs on the shoulder of the motorway when the traffic was in a lull, jumping up when a car or truck appeared on the horizon. Getting rides was easy. The truck drivers always stopped. It was always middle-aged men and they were always unfailingly kind. Even when I hitched alone up and down the island looking for work, and back in Israel, it was always middle-aged men, sometimes Arab farmers, and they were always kind. I learned this from hitchhiking with Eli—if you acted like strangers weren't dangerous, like they were friends offering help, they mostly responded in kind. I remembered Eli every time I stood on the asphalt shoulder, watching the trucks slow down, and then stop. He always greeted the drivers with surprise and graciousness, like they'd given him a gift. I tried to do the same. I'd been hitchhiking for months, sometimes alone, and the only trouble I'd had was during my trip with Ronnie to Sinai, when that soldier grabbed me.

Alastair and I were covering good distance on our way south until late afternoon, when our ride dropped us at a walled village along the highway. We stayed on the shoulder for what felt like hours. A car would blow by every fifteen or twenty minutes, and then they got further apart until traffic stopped all together. The town, the fields surrounding it, the highway, everything was silent. Even the birds had taken the afternoon off. The day was fading. There's no hitchhiking after dark; people who can't see you will not pick you up. We walked around looking for a restaurant, a guest house, anything open, any place to ask about camping for the night, or to buy food. But everything was shuttered tight. Was it a holiday? Was it a Sunday? It could have been. We never knew what time it was, much less what day.

I sat on the sidewalk with the packs, Alastair circled the town, then we switched places and I did the same. The houses were hidden behind high white stucco walls. The only sound came from the wind in the corn fields surrounding the village. The rows were tight against each other, the stalks strong like young trees, muddy dirt in what little space there was between them. We could not camp in the fields and it was cornfields as far as we could see. With each passing hour, it looked more like we would pass the night on the sidewalk, waiting for dawn and the next day's possibility of rides. The heat and silence grew heavy. We'd gone silent too. Words were not going to get us off the sidewalk.

An hour went by, two, the shadows got longer. A man appeared and beckoned for us to follow him. He was thin with dark hair, overdressed for the heat in long pants and a dark, long-sleeved shirt. He opened a gate in the wall and led us across a back courtyard. He showed us to a neat little room with a big lumpy bed and calendar pages taped to the wall. After showing us the bedroom, he led us under the back stairs of the main house to a little bathroom, the toilet flushed by filling a bucket and pouring the water into the bowl. We tried to give him some money, but he pulled his hands back, shook his head *no*. He disappeared and came back a few minutes later with a picnic in a paper bag—hard-boiled eggs, bread, strong cheese, oranges. We tried again to give him some money, and he again refused. He put his hands together in a prayer sign, said something we could not understand, and was gone. I felt like I had dreamed him. It wasn't obvious where he'd come from and when he left, out the gate of the courtyard, it wasn't clear where he was going. Early the next morning, we closed the gate behind as to walk the short distance back to the highway, and in no time, we were climbing into the cab of a semi-truck.

The old city in Athens, the Plaka, was where the cheap restaurants were, the divey little hotels. We found a room and spent a few days sightseeing. We walked up to the Acropolis and saw the remaining pillars, the big smooth stones in the ground on this plateau above the city. We wandered the narrow streets and got flatbread and olives and feta—we were always living on bread and cheese and olives—and once we ate in a restaurant with sidewalk tables. Alastair wanted to jump the low fence and skip out on the bill.

"Ask for the bathroom and head out the front instead" he said. "I'll meet you back at the pension."

I tried to imagine how this would work. People noticed me. If I disappeared the waiter would remember immediately that "American girl who looked like my cousin." Alastair stood out too, by contrast, so tall and skinny, so obviously English with his hard blue eyes.

Everywhere we went people were kind to me. They insisted I had to be Greek with my dark hair and my olive skin. I know it was just a pitch—mostly a pitch—but I didn't mind because they didn't want anything, just conversation in their Greek-accented English. Their attentions reminded me of the Israeli boys who wanted to take me home to their mothers, but without the annoyance of lust. The truck drivers, the restaurant owners, the soft-armed women behind cash registers in little corner shops, it felt like I was disappointing them when I insisted that, no, I was not Greek at all, not even a little bit. I wasn't going to let Alastair dine and dash on them. I refused. We fought when I insisted we pay the bill. He probably hit me later. I don't even remember.

Athens was much like Paris in that it was a thrill for me to see all this history in person. But it was harder to enjoy since we worried about money all the time. We needed to be working, not scraping our way across the continent. We needed a safe place to sleep and a way to feed ourselves that didn't involve stealing. The magical jobs that were supposed to appear in Greece had failed to materialize, leaving Alastair's hands bleeding and me unemployed. No matter what, Alastair was not going back to England. He insisted that was not an option. I was completely without direction or imagination about what to do next.

Returning to Israel was an easy solution. Once we got there, we were guaranteed to find work. Food and housing would be included. There were collective farms called *moshavs*. They were not quite collectives, but they were not fully private either. They had a sort of co-op system that was more commercial and bonus, they paid more than the *kibbutzim* did. Brian—the Texan from my language classes, the one with the drinking problem—had gone to one and we would see if he was still there, maybe work in the same place. We would blow most of the money from Alastair's father on ferry tickets to Israel, find the Texan with a drinking problem, and everything would fall into place after that. This was our plan to save ourselves. Blow all our money to return to a country in a perpetual state of war and find a drunk guy who would hook us up with work.

The ferry ran from Piraeus, the Athens port, to Haifa, the same port where Eli had boarded the ship for his adventures screwing European girls across the continent. The crossing took three days, and made two stops, one in Crete and one in Cyprus. On Crete, we walked up the hill to see the ruins of the palace, the place where the mythological Minotaur had been contained. I expected a real maze, one where you had to run a piece of string behind you so you could find your way out. It was mostly crumbling walls with a few faded frescoes and views over the choppy blue Mediterranean Sea. On Cyprus, the port was too far from the center of the city and Alastair did not want to pay for a taxi. Instead, we walked the seawall, smoking cigarettes and squinting into the distance, looking at the big ships headed off to everywhere.

Back on the ship, the forward deck was covered with backpackers, people too cheap or too rough or too stubborn to pay for a cabin. Our luck held; it did not rain. Though one night the sea rolled enough to wake me from my sleep. For a while, I watched the stars shift right to left and back again. It felt like the sky was moving while we were perfectly still underneath it.

CHAPTER FOURTEEN:
Back to the Land

Brian was living in a ramshackle cabin on a *moshav* in northern Israel. The *moshav* had no cafeteria, no communal housing. Just a few old buildings the residents had left behind for workers when they built their own, more luxurious homes. We didn't have to pay for housing and food was cheap because we could eat well from things that were grown on the farm. For more processed things, like dairy and pasta, there was a community shop that sold everything we might need. And since it was part of the co-op, prices were low. If you were smart and did not blow all your money on alcohol, like Brian did, you could save quite a bit of cash.

My first job was as a housekeeper, scrubbing bathrooms and vacuuming and washing dishes in the kosher double kitchen of a religious family. The work was less demanding than field work, but I did not enjoy it. I spent every Friday morning helping a talkative and cheerful woman prepare her house for the Sabbath. She was patient with my Hebrew and her kids were polite enough, if a bit bossy. It felt weird to be treated like the help, but I was grateful for the work, for the neatly folded bills this woman placed in my hand every week before sending me home. And it was good for my conversational skills. I wasn't a good housekeeper. The work was hard for me to do well because I couldn't make myself care about how well I'd scrubbed a shower. I wanted to be outside.

We had arrived during the banana harvest season. Harvesting bananas required a lot of physical strength. I was not strong enough to carry the big bunches when they were cut from the trees, and I was not tall enough to make the cuts. Alastair was working as a mule, supporting the heavy bunches of green bananas while the farmer he worked for sliced them free from the trees. Alastair loaded the heavy bunches onto a trailer, then the two of them drove to a warehouse where the crop would get weighed and shipped off to market. It was intensely physical work, but Alastair liked it well enough. It beat hauling buckets of concrete, paid more, and we had a much better place to live.

When the harvest was over, a job opened for me in the fields with Alastair's banana farmer. I eagerly quit housekeeping and went to work outside. Alastair's farmer was an English immigrant with several acres of fields. His workers did farm labor while he ran his business—something to do with graphic design—out of his home.

I loved walking in the banana orchards. The trees were weird brightly colored succulents, so strange in their shape. And the fields had that smell of banana peels, but not like they'd gone brown—somehow brighter, sharper. I loved the stiff smooth leaves and the alien-like buds and flowers, and the crunch of the dead leaves underfoot. Working in the banana fields meant a lot of walking while carrying a very big knife, and that felt badass. Much of the work involved trimming shoots from around the base of hundreds of banana trees. I spent all day walking in this strange, low forest of smooth off-kilter trees, swinging a big knife in one hand. I'd twist the knife in the ground, carve out the smaller shoots around the strongest trunk, then move on to circling the next tree. Alastair and I spent much of our time in silence, or listening to the radio, sometimes stopping to admire the blue sky through the frame of all these bright green leaves.

One day I found a chameleon, his eyes rotating in opposite directions. I gently picked him up and placed him in a blue bucket to see if he would turn blue. He did not, so I put him on the ground among the big brown leaves, and he faded until he matched his more natural background. I learned how to drive an old tractor, Elizabeth—she had a name—and I loved that too, the clunk of the old engine, the touchy clutch. The farmer was very protective of this machine. He'd kept it running well past its life span, and it frustrated him that I would grind the gears. I finally learned to get Elizabeth to behave, finally learned how to feel the drop point, to get her to hum along the hard-packed dirt road out to the orchards. She was rusty red with a tall narrow grill. When the farmer drove, Alastair and I would perch on the fenders over her tall back wheels.

Our farmer was kind and patient when I was not grinding the clutch on his tractor. He was easy about days off when the weather was bad or if we wanted a night in the city. He invited us for dinner now and again, or for lunch on Shabbat. Best of all, he was generous with his English-language library as long as I delivered on my promise to return his books when I was done. He was an odd bird, never married but not gay, either, just one of those bookish bachelors who never finds a mate. I liked him, but on days when the work seemed tedious or the heat was oppressive, we talked trash about him being lazy for not joining us in the fields. After all, it was his land; shouldn't he be working it too? We did not know exactly how he spent his time when he was not with us. We imagined him drinking iced tea and sitting in his cool shuttered rooms while we sweltered surrounded by his bright green trees. Most days, though, he was just a guy who had another job.

One weekend Alastair and I went to Jerusalem to stay with a friend he'd met when he first got to Israel. Eileen was American, smart and pretty and Jewish. She and Alastair had become friends when she was studying Hebrew with the previous group of students at the kibbutz where I'd learned. She had stayed on to take classes at the Hebrew University. She shared an apartment with a couple, an American woman and an English guy, and they were funny and smart and kind. Meeting Eileen and her roommates made me realize how lonely I'd been living on the *moshav* with just Brian and Alastair for conversation, and how much I missed Ronnie.

At first, I was bitterly jealous of Eileen's easy friendship with Alastair, though neither of them gave me a reason to feel this way. Eileen had an Israeli boyfriend, and nothing had ever happened between her and Alastair. She seemed so together, with her excellent Hebrew and her nice student boyfriend and her cool, well-traveled roommates. I was sick with envy for their cheaply furnished apartment, their group dinners, their student lives. Everything looked so appealing to me, all the good-natured conversations, the bright spaces filled with Jerusalem daylight, the bus rides to classes at the university. I sulked the first day we were there. I wanted everything they had so badly.

Eileen took us to meet a classmate who lived on campus and had a room that was basically a closet. We all shoehorned ourselves in there and smoked cigarettes and practiced our Hebrew slang while Alastair looked at us like we were strangers. He never did take to the language. It's not like he expected everyone to speak English, but he didn't make any effort to speak Hebrew, either. He threw that on me, always. I bought the bus tickets, I made the bargains in the markets,

I did the ordering whenever we were in a restaurant. I did all the talking.

While we were in Jerusalem, we took the bus to Bethlehem with Eileen's roommates to have tea with a Palestinian family they had made friends with. We sat in their stone house drinking glasses of mint tea and eating triangular pieces of perfect baklava. We did not talk about politics, even though between us we had enough Hebrew to do so. We went for a walk and peeked into the place where Joseph and Mary supposedly found shelter the night Jesus was born. I was surprised to find it was more a cave than a stable, as the story tells us.

Bethlehem was a pile of golden stone behind another stone wall, the surrounding hillsides terraced with olive and lemon trees, little winding dirt roads going up to homesteads where there were goats in pens and kids playing in yards. I could not connect these people to the fighters shooting rockets over the border when I had been on kibbutz. This quiet man and his solicitous wife—he in an immaculate white shirt, she in an immaculate white scarf—they treated us like honored guests while we sat there in our farm clothes. They were simply neighbors making tea for people who had dropped by for the afternoon.

When the weekend was over, I wanted to stay with Eileen in the city, to tell her everything about Alastair, about how he was hurting me, and how I was lost and didn't know what to do about it. I kept looking for someone to rescue me, as though they could see what I was living with even though I never said a word. How was Eileen supposed to know Alastair hit me if I didn't tell her? And if I had would she believe what I said? They were friends. Would she take Alastair's side if it came to that? As usual, I said nothing, and I was sad when we took the bus back to the farm. It felt like watching another escape hatch clang shut as the city grew smaller in the distance.

The season turned. The rains came. Some days we couldn't work because the fields were too wet, the rain too disruptive. I cooked in the makeshift kitchen on the propane stove, and Brian drank all the time and got weird to be around. Out of nowhere, he would say things that were mean or hinted at violence, and I started to avoid him. I kept to myself, reading my way through our farmer's library until another American worker showed up and then I read all her books too. She got mad at me because I creased the spine on her copy of *The Source*, a fat James Michener historical novel about an archeological site in northern Israel. We spent these unplanned days drinking coffee and looking out the front door at the rain, avoiding making any plans. Then the season ended, and we found a posting on a Negev farm, also a co-op, where the pay was better and the housing was nice. The work was the hardest yet.

The farm had acres and acres of tomatoes. We lay out rows of black plastic, and then we cut holes in the plastic and planted each tomato seedling by hand. We ran the drip irrigation lines, placing the dripper valves right next to the fragile stems. The plastic would hold the water in the ground during the day and keep the plants warm at night—the desert nights could be cold. As the plants grew, we used clippers to cut the weak stems off so the strongest ones could carry the most fruit. One day, in a fit of anger, Alastair threw his clippers at me and they punctured my thigh. I sat on the fender of the tractor trying not to cry as he drove me to the clinic.

"What happened?" asked the doctor.

"It was an accident," I said, as though that were enough. I waited for him to ask more questions, for anyone to ask more questions, but it never happened. It was an accident; that was enough. I felt so stupid, like a terrible cliché. I'd walked into a door. I tripped while carrying something. I slipped on the stairs.

What happened? Alastair hurt me again, that's what happened. It was the first time he'd drawn blood, so that was notable. If I told the doctor what had happened, would he even care? Every time I was on the edge of telling someone what had happened, what was still happening, I stalled out. I was scared that if I started talking, I would not be able to stop. I was scared whoever I told would find a way to make it be my fault. "It was an accident," I said, and the doctor did not press me.

There was no shade in the fields, just some thin scrubby trees that did nothing to keep the heat off. I found a dog, a little patchwork puppy. I took him back and forth with me to the fields for about a week, feeding him on the front porch, playing with him after our workday was done. I didn't bring him in at night, but he was always waiting outside when we headed to work in the morning. One day he ate rat poison—the fields were full of toxic stuff to keep the animals off the plants. He died, shaking, foam coming out of his mouth as I held him. I cried, heartbroken to see him snuffed out, even though he had no future here. He was small and sweet and young. But I could not watch him every moment when I was working, and he did not know any better. We buried him under the scrubby trees and not a day passed that I did not walk by that spot and miss him.

For the first part of the season we lived in a row house, much like the one I first lived in when I arrived in the country. There were Arab workers bunked here too. They did not—or would not—speak Hebrew and we did not work together. In the evenings they would lounge out front smoking cigarettes and eating canned sardines and bread while sitting on the trailer of the tractor they drove to and from their fields. Our other neighbors were three funny, cheerful American guys and I liked their company.

On our days off Alastair and I would wander out into the desert, beyond the old firing range signs and stare into the sand colored distance. Sometimes we would take our clothes off and lie on the warm rocks. I wrote home and told my dad about how Alastair had thrown his clippers at me. I wrote the words on the page and told him the facts of the story, and life just went on like usual. My dad didn't write, he didn't call, nothing happened. It was the closest I'd come to asking for help, to telling anyone that Alastair was abusing me. But even when I wrote it down on the page, it didn't seem real because nothing happened to stop it. I was either crazy or I deserved the treatment I was getting. Or maybe everyone expected me to deal with it myself, as though I knew what to do in this situation.

Our farmer was a short, talkative man. His wife was tall and lean and mostly silent, which wasn't surprising given how much her husband talked. They built a nice studio cabin behind their home and moved us into it, away from the Arab farm workers. Our new neighbors were an English guy and his girlfriend, a very pretty young black girl from Trinidad. Her boyfriend was awful to her. He said horrible racist things, insulted her, called her stupid, and bossed her around. It was shocking to watch, and I saw myself in it too. I wanted to tell her, "I know, I know, we should run away together, let's get out of here," but it felt useless. I could not take care of her. I could not help her. I could not help myself.

"Do you see the way he treats her?" I asked Alastair, wondering if he would see himself.

"She is kind of stupid," he said. I did not mention bring it up again.

Our new boss did not like us much. He found us antisocial and ungrateful and he told us so on more than one occasion. Once, the family went away and left us the keys to their house so we could watch TV. When they got back, he told us we'd left the house a mess; his wife had complained. I had to wrack my brain to see how that could be. We had gone inside, yes, and we had watched TV, but he complained that the living room was full of sand.

Sand was everywhere, all the time. It was the desert. Sand would blow in under the doors and through the window screens. Yes, we were antisocial. It was because I was so ashamed of what was happening when no one could see us. I wanted to tell him I needed help; maybe he could help my neighbor too. We both needed rescuing because neither of us had the strength to rescue ourselves. Again, I was silent. I apologized to the farmer. I apologized to his wife. I said we must have let the wind bring the sand in, it was my fault, I am so sorry.

There were turkeys here—big, hot coops full of turkeys. We did not have to pack them like crops, but we did have to vaccinate them. It was not as bad as harvesting chickens. By the time you'd dropped the turkey after jabbing it with a needle and injecting the serum into their fat legs, they'd forgotten they were fighting you. They turkeys were ugly and stupid, but they were also only chicks, so their strength to hurt you was limited.

On Thanksgiving, Alastair butchered a turkey for dinner. He killed the bird, and I pulled the feathers off the carcass and prepared as traditional a dinner as possible with what I had on hand. I wanted to do something that reminded me of home. With all these turkeys around, Thanksgiving dinner was an obvious choice. I used the oven in the main house—the family was away again—and when it was done cooking I had a picture-perfect bird. Alastair, in a fit of anger about god knows what, threw the whole browned bird out the front door of our cabin into the rain and wet sand. I did not have the heart to go get it. I crawled into bed, pulled the blankets over my head, and cried until I fell asleep. The next morning, I tossed the battered turkey in the trash, untouched.

After months of tending to the tomato plants, we were instructed to destroy them. It turned out to be more profitable to take a loss than it was to sell the crop. We pulled up the very plants we'd placed in the ground with both hands. We shook the tomatoes off into big plastic bins and left the plants on the ground. The bins would get weighed—here's how many pounds, how many tons of tomatoes you grew but did not sell this year—and then emptied into the landfill. Once the field was stripped bare of fruit, we pulled up the plastic and threw that away too. The only thing that we saved was the irrigation, which we pulled apart, rolled up, and stored in a barn. It was dirty work. We were covered in pulp and sand. It was also demoralizing to throw our entire season of work away. The harvest would have been hard work too, but we would literally have seen the fruits of our labor when it was over. Instead, everything went into the trash, the plants, the rotting fruit, the plastic sheeting, everything but the irrigation system.

When we were done tearing out the tomato crops, I found out my birth control had failed. I was pregnant.

Alastair was furious. "I've been here before," he said, "you're trying to trap me." Nothing could have been further from the truth. I was the one who was trapped. "You're not fucking keeping it," he hissed at me.

I laughed at his assumptions. I had made a lot of mistakes because I didn't know what to do, but this time, I knew right away what had to happen: I needed to get an abortion. I called Eileen in Jerusalem. She immediately became the friend I needed.

"Don't worry," she said on the phone. "I'll help you get it taken care of."

Abortion was legal and easy enough to get, Eileen told me. I would need to see a doctor—Eileen would find out where and how—and they would approve the procedure. Or not, depending on my health. She assured me it would be no problem, and that she had friends who had been through it. She would find out everything, I just needed to come back to Jerusalem.

It was time to go anyway. Our farmers were increasingly frustrated with us for not being the cheerful, gracious workers they'd had last harvest season. We'd never be as good as they were. It would have been wearing thin even if I hadn't been at the whims of Alastair's vicious temper. "You have no idea," I thought, while listening yet again to stories of the sunny, near family workers they'd traded in for us. We packed up what few belongings we had and hitchhiked north to Jerusalem and Eileen. She made me an appointment at the hospital right after we arrived.

The doctor was brief and direct. "About six weeks," he declared, and told me to come back in three days to have the abortion. Early the next morning, I woke up with searing cramps. I locked myself in the bathroom in Eileen's apartment and blood spilled out of me, followed by a wad of lumpy tissue. I woke Alastair and we took a taxi to the hospital. I'd miscarried.

I was awash in relief. I spent a day in the hospital, dragging around an IV and sleeping. I again thought about my high school friend Casey, back in California. No, Idaho. It would have been Idaho. That's where she'd been sent to deal with her "mistake." It seemed like she had no choice in what happened after she got pregnant. Her parents stepped in and made all the decisions. She would have the baby; she would put it up for adoption. Afterwards, she would finish up high school in some private girls' school that I imagined had high fences around it and severe teachers in military style uniforms. My other friend—the one who'd been having sex in the park bathroom with that homeless guy—she had no choice either. Her parents decided what they wanted her to do; they didn't even ask her.

I was embarrassed that I'd been so uncharitable when Casey wrote me her story. At the time, I was so angry that she had let this happen to her. I did not understand that birth control failure could happen to anyone. Miss a dose or two. Take antibiotics. Buy your birth control from a pharmacy in the Jerusalem street market, not a licensed pharmacy or clinic, to save money. Maybe that was the problem. Whatever the cause, it could happen.

I wanted to write to Casey and tell her I was sorry. Sorry it had taken me so long to write back and sorry about what she had been through. But the only address I had for her was in California, and I did not want to contact her parents. I was worried that if I wrote to her at the address I had, her parents would not forward my letters— or worse, they would read them before throwing them away. They would judge me again, and I did not want that.

I spent the night in the hospital. The next morning, I was rolled into an operating room where, under full anesthesia, a doctor cleaned what was left of the messy cells out of me and then, a day later, sent me home. Alastair came to get me. We walked to the bus stop because he did not want to pay for a taxi. We squeezed on to a crowded bus and I stood, lightheaded and weak, hanging from the strap as the bus lurched through the narrow streets of Jerusalem back to Eileen's apartment.

Eileen gave us her room and went to stay with her boyfriend. She came and hung out with me every day while I recovered. She plied me with cookies and soup and tea and stories. The bleeding had stopped just two or three days after I'd been released, and I felt fine. I was relieved not to have had the abortion, but I suppose I was hair-splitting. I had made up my mind to get an abortion; I was not conflicted. It felt like I got off easy since I didn't have to choose.

I kept thinking about Alastair saying, "You're not fucking keeping it," as though that were even the merest wisp of an option. This bitter young man who I had anchored myself to thought I would want to have a baby with him? Ridiculous. I didn't understand why I was with him, only that I did not know what else to do. The idea that I'd want him to father a child with me was laughable.

A week went by and it was obvious that I was fine—physically, at least. It was time to go. Alastair and I were both tired of the work, and it had filled our wallets enough to move on. We bought bus tickets south for Eilat, a beach resort town on the Red Sea. In Eilat, we would change get a bus to Sharm El Sheikh on the very end of the Sinai Peninsula. There, we would board a ferry to Hurghada on the Egyptian side of the Suez Gulf and then take the bus to Cairo.

When it came time to say goodbye to Eileen, I burst into tears. No one had been nice to me for what seemed like so long, nice to me in a way that made me feel truly cared for. I fell apart. I was so embarrassed, but I couldn't stop crying. She wiped my tears away with her bare hands and hugged me hard. Alastair watched as I continued to cry for all the things I could not say out loud. I couldn't find the words to tell Eileen how thankful I was that she'd promised me I wouldn't be stuck pregnant. I cried with gratitude for her support. I cried because I was afraid of what was next, but I didn't know how to change direction.

I could not speak up, and I could not go home. I had no other ideas. So I stopped crying and walked to the bus stop with Alastair, and we headed towards Cairo.

CHAPTER FIFTEEN:
A Second Passport

It was a liability, traveler's wisdom said, to have an Israeli stamp in your passport. This traveler's wisdom—we relied on it all the time though I could not tell you where exactly we picked it up. It did not help us when we went to Greece looking for work, but we hadn't learned. We relied on it all the same.

Word was it was bad enough to be an American traveling east of Europe, but to be an American with Israel marked all over your passport was worse. Word was that India—our end goal—would not issue you a visa if you showed up at the embassy with a passport covered in Israeli visas. Word was you could get a second passport issued from the American embassy in Cairo and use that for traveling in parts of the world that were vehemently anti-Israel. Egypt would be our launch pad to nations in the east, a steppingstone on the way to India. But first, we had to stop in Cairo and get new passports.

Transiting the Sinai this last time filled me with nostalgia. The peninsula was in the news a lot; stories about what would happen once it went back to Egypt were conflicting. Sometimes we heard it

137

would be developed for tourism, something the Israelis had not done much. Other times we heard the Egyptians were blowing up the reefs to eliminate mines the Israeli military had supposedly anchored in the waters. All of it broke my heart a little because Sinai was where I'd slept under the stars with Eli, where Ronnie and I had coffee every morning just out of the sun in the doorway of our palm leaf shack. I wanted Sinai to stay like I remembered it forever. Like I could always be sitting on the beach reading or wading on the patches of sand between the coral, knee deep in the clear shallow waters, brightly colored fish just below the surface.

The port at Sharm El Sheikh was a cinder block building on a flat dry arrowhead of land. There were some oil tankers offshore, a few dusty trailers. The town felt empty, temporary. There must have been a village somewhere, but we did not visit it. We lingered in the shade of the barebones ferry terminal until it was time to board.

The ferry was a passenger boat with benches under an awning and a small cabin. There were no other Western travelers, just Egyptian and Israeli businessmen and rugged blue-collar workers. The ferry took us across the channel, along the towering hulls of container ships and oil tankers. At the top of the gangplank on the other side, we boarded a bus to Cairo. The bus felt downright luxurious, with its reclining seats and window curtains. I'd been used to the rattling beat-up Israeli buses, which had no amenities. I pushed the curtains aside and looked out the window at the countryside—date palms, beehive-shaped clay ovens, villages behind mud brick walls. There were people working in the same kind of fields I'd worked in, cotton and citrus, under bleached out skies.

The bus dropped us in the middle of Cairo. I'd picked up a secondhand guidebook in Israel; we used it to locate a recommended cheap traveler's hotel. We found our way through a city that was loud and strangely dark brown—the buildings, the light, the buses and cars. It was as if everything was made of walnut. There was stone and concrete and, hell, there were new modern apartment and office buildings, but somehow, everything seemed the same color, everything filtered through a spilled coffee light.

To get to the hotel we had to go up a wide flight of spiral stairs to the second floor in one of these brown buildings, built in the 1930s or 1940s. There was a small cage elevator with a rattling gate, but I did not trust it. The hotel lobby was open to the stairwell. To the right, there was a tall reception desk, and behind it a quiet man who gave us a key from a mailbox cubby and wrote the price of the room on a scrap of newsprint.

The hotel was a strange dream—also brown, like Cairo outside, but quiet, muffled, the light softened by yellowed window glass. Everything was sepia-colored, like an old photograph, the walls, the windows, the curtains... The ceilings were high to help keep the heat down, and the halls were lined with big, heavy brown furniture, as though a store had gone out of business and there was nowhere else for these battered armoires, dressers, and bedposts to go. Nearly every horizontal surface was covered with piles of faded Arabic language newspapers.

If there were other guests besides a trio of talkative German guys, we didn't know about them; we never saw anybody else. The German guys had been robbed a few weeks back in Sudan. We hung out with them in the street-level restaurant downstairs drinking light Egyptian beer, eating plates of *fuul*—fava bean stew—and pita bread, and talking about travel. The German guys wore leather pants and had almost no belongings. They'd been driving a Land Rover south when they'd been stopped by armed Sudanese rebels who took their car and left them at the side of the road with little more than the clothes they'd been wearing. They did not fight, the German guys said. Why would they? They were unarmed, and there was no point. They handed over their car keys and sat on the side of the road until someone drove by. They had hitchhiked back to Cairo and were hanging out at this empty hotel trying to figure out what to do next. They weren't broke, but their plans to drive the length of Africa to Cape Town were interrupted. They were in good spirits for people who had been carjacked on a desert highway. Maybe they were rich kids? Or maybe they'd had nothing to lose when they set out, so this was just another story in their adventure.

Urban Cairo disappeared into the desert shortly before the Great Pyramids. We took the bus out to see them, these giant structures that made me laugh, so exactly like I had always imagined them, and more impressive at the same time. It was strange to recognize them so completely and to be so surprised by the idea that they were real. I ran my fingers down the seams where the giant stone blocks sat tight against each other and they felt familiar and warm. Anytime we encountered an iconic work of art—the Great Pyramids, the *Mona Lisa*, the Acropolis in Athens—I was bright with the joy of recognition. Seeing any of the masterworks, from the modest sized Leonardo painting to the massive stone pyramids, was like greeting a friend I didn't know I'd missed so much.

The Sphinx sat quietly in the low sandstone trench in which she'd been built. We walked around the edges at about her shoulder level, admiring her distinctive profile, her neatly shaped paws, and her powerful lioness body. I knew her already from history classes and now here she was, right in front of me, her broken nose taking nothing from her strength.

Here and there hawkers asked if we wanted camel rides. We stayed on foot and wandered around—and into—the monumental tombs. We were alone in one of them, with only the attendant, and he gestured towards Alastair that he could climb into the empty, lidless sarcophagus. Alastair declined.

The next day we wandered the cavernous and uncrowded Egyptian Museum through gallery after vast gallery stuffed with stunning artifacts, painted coffins, stone relief carvings, gold and lapis lazuli jewelry and scarabs and staffs. The kohl-lined eyes of past Egyptian royalty watched us drift past their treasures, and our footsteps echoed in the dimly lit rooms. Every now and then we'd encounter a khaki-clad guard, who would nod our way, silent as the statues. Maybe there'd be another pair of tourists, reflected on a glass case that held a gold leafed headdress, and then, we'd lose sight of them. I didn't understand why there weren't more people here. Athens had been a hive of tourists, Paris the same. Cairo, home to the pyramids, the Sphinx, and the treasures of the pharaohs—King Tut's death mask with its blue and gold mane, the bust of Nefertiti's elegant face—was bursting with people, but tourists seemed nonexistent.

As promised, getting new passports was a simple administrative task. We filled out paperwork, handed over our street-corner passport photos. Mine were blown out—there were dark shadows where my eyes were, my face was featureless and pale. The pictures were completely unacceptable, and the embassy took them, no questions asked, along with my application. I paid my fee and was told it would take a few days, come back in a week. Alastair did the same at the British embassy. Then we went to see the city. We left downtown Cairo and the light opened up. The sky was bright blue, and the buildings were the pale, creamy color of sand.

We took a local bus to the end of the line and walked out on a hot dry road to see the Coptic churches. I didn't know what the Copts were, but I had seen pictures of the icon paintings, saints with dark skin and almond eyes backed by gold-leaf halos, and I wanted to be in their presence. So off we went. We had no idea how far the walk was to the churches from the end of the bus line, and we were used to Israel, where you could always get a ride. A taxi came along and picked us up—it was cheap—and dropped us in a quiet complex where a monk in black robes took us to wash our hands before leading us a chapel full of exactly the icons I'd wanted to see.

We had not made any plans for the return trip and as we set back out in the afternoon sun, I wondered if we could make the walk all the way back to where we'd got off the bus. It was hot, there were no cars, and Alastair was becoming angry. Out of nowhere, a car rolled to a halt beside us and the driver asked us if we needed a ride. We were so grateful, and the driver seemed amused to find us. He would not take the money I insisted Alastair offer him.

A day or so later, we went to Alexandria, because of the name. I knew it had been home to a library once, one of the great wonders of the ancient world. I had imagined there would be remains for us to see. I was wrong, there was nothing to see, no reason we could find to be there as tourists. We became hopelessly lost in the back streets while looking for something, anything that would help us make sense of our choice to come to this city. Boys playing in the streets pulled up their long white galabia to mock Alastair's shorts as though he was walking around in his underwear. Away from the center of town he must have looked crazy, half-dressed, far from anywhere an outsider should be. We wandered in circles until we found someone who spoke

English though all he could say was, "I'm sorry, I cannot help you." I do not remember how we found our way back into the center of town, but we got a hotel and walked on the beach until sunset.

We were so out of place, always dressed wrong, wandering around looking at everything like we had never seen buildings or cars or people before, when really, we were the ones who were strange. While we were looking for a place to get dinner, a man stalked us down side streets and alleys, and finally, Alastair turned and confronted him.

"Why are you following us?" His anger was right on the surface. I wondered if he would take a swing at this stranger.

"I just wanted to talk to you," the man said. His English was good, clear. He looked scared.

"I don't want to talk to you." Alastair threw the words at him and pulled me away down the street. I looked back and the man hadn't moved. His shoulders slumped inside his clean white shirt. I was washed in a wave of sadness. He was curious but did not know how to break the ice with us. My guess is he had been trying to work up the nerve to say something. What he had been doing was creepy, but when I looked at him, he appeared harmless. So many strangers had been kind so far, I didn't think he would be any different, given the chance. Alastair was not going to give him one, though.

Back in Cairo we went to the central station to buy train tickets to Luxor. Afterwards, we had a fight on a pedestrian overpass and when Alastair pulled me close to apologize, some men yelled at us to take that behavior back to our own country. Men and women did not show affection in public, it was simply not done. Women were a miniscule percentage of who I saw out on the streets. Young women were not out on the streets in the company of young men ever, not with their hair flying free, not with their legs bare. I saw couples, some, walking side by side. The women wore long skirts and long sleeves, their heads covered in scarves. They were stylish, with makeup and jewelry, but so modest. It was pairs of men who walked around holding hands, in their white shirts and dark pants.

I was another species entirely. Women did not behave as I did in Egypt. It would not have been considered respectable. I was constantly out of place. Once, a young man stopped me on the street to ask me about my t-shirt—it had the Hebrew name of my kibbutz on it. It was the rare moment that I was out alone. I had gone to buy postcards and stamps at a shop around the corner from the hotel. The young man had been to Israel, and his English was good. I greeted him with suspicion at first, not only because of what had happened in Alexandria.

On the streets of Cairo, I was clearly not a "good" woman. Men would shout after me, press up against me on the bus. I had taken to asking Alastair to stand in front of me, to use his body like a shield to keep the men from putting their hands on me. The streets were okay, the shouting just turned into noise, but I hated taking the bus because it was not just staring, it was much more. Hands were everywhere, and once, a man pressed his lips on my arm as I hung onto the rail to keep myself upright. I could have disappeared here easily enough—a black scarf, a modest blouse, a long skirt. I might have looked like any of the Egyptian women, but it did not occur to me to do so, and was no guarantee it would have helped. I dressed as modestly I could with what I had, but it was not enough. I took a deep breath and turned to answer something the young man had asked me. He really did just want to talk. He asked me what I had been doing in Israel, told me he had worked there and had fond memories of it, and wished me safe travels.

The train to Luxor was quiet and clean; we were the roughest looking people in the car. A young girl ran up and down the aisle playing with a bright green parakeet and smiling. The bird was docile, clearly attached to her, and hopped in and out of her hands. Her family looked at us and smiled, shaking their heads indulgently. In the town of Luxor we rented bicycles to see the towering statues of the pharaohs, the hieroglyph-covered tombs, the tulip columns, the partially excavated obelisks.

This ancient city on the banks of the Nile was absent of visitors, just as vacant as the Egyptian Museum in Cairo. We rode our rattling bicycles up the hot open avenues of what was once Thebes with only the silent statues of long dead queens and kings for company. The sky was so blue, the carvings still so sharp. I carried a bundle of cheap newsprint and made pencil rubbings of the reliefs, the scarab-shaped seals and the profile of a princess with perfect braids, each twist of her hair carved in exquisite detail.

At the entrance to each tomb we would trade a stack of battered piasters for a printed ticket. Then the attendant would turn a broken scrap of mirror to reflect the sunlight from outside into the fresco-covered chambers. The light was imperfect. There were dark corners into which we could not see. The rooms were empty save for the paintings on the walls and maybe, in the middle, a heavy stone coffin emptied of its occupant. The objects I'd seen at the museum in Cairo, or the British Museum in London, this is where they'd come from, these cool stone rooms. It's where they were meant to be still, hidden behind the sandy, crenellated cliffs, were it not for archeologists and thieves waking the pharaohs from thousands of years of sleep to steal their jewelry. The avenues were lined with towering columns and nothing seemed quite real, including the silence. Maybe we'd see another pair of visitors, over there, but then they'd disappear into the shadows of the massive columns at the Karnak temple complex. How could we have this place to ourselves? Where was everyone?

The Germans were still in the traveler's hotel when we returned to Cairo from Luxor. They had made plans and like us had set their sights on India. But there was another administrative hurdle. Getting a visa to India meant mailing those fresh passports off and waiting for who knows how long for them to come back. I was not keen on spending more time in Cairo than I had to. There was the relentless brown light, the noise, and it was getting to me that I could not do anything or go anywhere without being harassed.

There was a faster way to get a visa, the Germans told us, though you'd have to buy a plane ticket. You could fly to Karachi, Pakistan, where a getting a visa meant a quick visit to the Indian embassy, passport in hand. You'd have it that same day. Then you could travel overland by train to Lahore, crossing into India in Punjab—in the north. If you were brave or foolish, you could travel overland to Pakistan from Egypt, but it meant crossing Iraq and Iran. The two countries were at war, and the Ayatollah's oppressive government was in control of Iran.

For a few hundred dollars, we could fly east and leapfrog all of that. We'd land in Pakistan where what money we had would go even farther than it had in Israel or Egypt. We decided spending the money was a better idea than tackling the Iran–Iraq border. We went to a travel agent and bought plane tickets to Karachi. We took the bus from downtown Cairo to the airport. We had money for a cab, but Alastair never wanted to pay for something that was easy when the hard way was so cheap.

CHAPTER SIXTEEN:
Off the Map

We landed in Karachi at sundown, cleared immigration, and took a taxi to a hotel on the beach. It was a dive of a place with a high wall around the outside. The rooms faced an interior courtyard. There was a weak fan in the middle of the ceiling, a low-wattage light, and a bathroom where the bare concrete floor never dried. The beach, a wide curve of dark brown sand, was not far from the entrance of the hotel. There was a shipwreck just offshore. If we'd wanted to, we could have waded out to touch what was left of the rusting hull. There were a few boys, maybe eight years old, maybe ten, running on the sand in the fading light.

It felt like since leaving Israel, I was always seeing little boys, but never girls. And the women I saw were either so obviously possessions of their husbands or beyond the interest of men entirely. They were grandmothers sweeping walkways or babysitters for those boys allowed to run free in front of them. They were never their own people, never women alone without men.

Early the next morning, after I'd given up swatting mosquitoes for the night, I dressed in shorts and a t-shirt, and tried to walk out on the beach again, alone.

"You cannot leave here like that," the guard at the entrance to the hotel compound said. "You cannot." He was perched on a stool just outside the front gate.

"What do you mean?" I asked.

"You cannot leave here like that," he said again. His English was perfect. He waved his hand towards my bare legs.

I finally realized what he was saying. I blushed, I was so embarrassed. The Lonely Planet guidebook I had picked up was for India; I had no context for Pakistan. I did not know I was supposed to be covered until this man at the gate of the hotel told me, in his understated way.

We'd arrived at night, I'd seen nothing of the people here, and I had completely forgotten where I was. I went back to my room and dressed in the most modest things I had, a baggy t-shirt and my skirt. It still was not enough, but it would have to do. My head remained uncovered. I walked on the beach alone for a while. There were more boys running on the sand, the shipwreck just offshore, the tide higher than it had been the night before. Freighters bobbed on the horizon, and not far up the coastline, was downtown Karachi.

Alastair and I walked to the Indian embassy that same morning. Along the approach to the embassy gates, the sidewalks were lined with men squatting in front of typewriters. For a few rupees they would fill out your visa application on an old Smith Corona or Royal, the kind with a steeply angled keyboard, the keys in a tight semicircle in front of the roller. They were all busy. There seemed to be a tremendous demand for their service. The clatter of typewriter keys filled the street.

Getting our visas meant handing over the fee, the paperwork, and looking the officer in the eye. It took no more time than mailing a letter. The line for us was non-existent. We were in and out in minutes while the line for Pakistanis stretched on and on and on.

With no information about what to do now that we were in Karachi, we were completely at loose ends. It was hot, so we sat in the air-conditioned lobby of the Karachi Hilton reading the English-language newspapers provided by the hotel for its guests. No one asked us why we were there, though we were woefully underdressed compared to everyone else, Alastair in shorts and a t-shirt, me in my wrap skirt, my lower legs bare. We were white, though, so of course we went unquestioned. The hotel lobby lacked any sense of place; we could have been anywhere in the world. The marbled receptionist counter, the shiny metal coffee tables with glass tops, the towering lobby atrium—were we in Karachi or Kansas City? The only indicator that we were in Pakistan was the predominance of hotel guests, men with black hair and crisp white shirts. Every overheard conversation was like any imagined international business conversation anywhere. *How was your flight? Are you prepared for the meeting? Did you get the contract I sent you?*

Bored with the hotel lobby and with no idea what to do until we could get a train to the Indian border the next day, we wandered. There was a big white monument up the hill. We headed that direction to find out what it was. We had not been walking long when a man pulled his car over on to the shoulder and asked us if he could show us around. We looked at each other and looked at him. "It's so rare I see young foreign travelers," he said. "I promise you, I mean no harm, I would just like to talk and show you my city." We traded a look, Alastair and I, and in it was the man who had stalked us around Alexandria. But the man was so direct, and we decided to trust him.

Alastair got in the front seat and I climbed in back and this man, with no agenda at all, drove us around Karachi, stopping the car at various historical monuments. The mausoleum where Pakistan's founder is buried. A modernist mosque from the 1960s. Alastair knew a little about Pakistani politics—there had been a military coup, the elected leader was in prison. And while in the front seat Alastair and the stranger talked about what would happen with Pakistan, I stared out the window at the city streets. The women I saw were fully covered, head to toe. Even their faces were hidden. They looked like cartoon ghosts in blue or black. I wondered if they were wearing shorts and t-shirts underneath. I wondered if it was more convenient to not be seen, given what I'd experienced in Egypt, given that I stood out so much here. Would my travels have been easier if I'd been covered?

Our unofficial guide bought us lunch, spicy curry and Coke in glass bottles, and then returned us to our hotel, wishing us safe and happy travels. He pressed a business card on Alastair and told him to get in touch should we come back through Karachi. He would be grateful to help us out. Alastair tossed the card in the plastic wastebasket as soon as we entered our hotel room. It felt like a callous move, but we both knew we weren't coming back. We had never intended on coming here in the first place.

We walked to the train station at first light. I bought the train tickets. The crowds were fifteen, twenty people deep at the ticket window. But there was a line for women. "I got this," I told Alastair, and went to by two tickets for Lahore, near the border with India. We walked out on to the platform to wait for our train.

The train appeared and the station was a chaotic swirl of people and noise and chaos. I couldn't wait to board. It was not that I was keen to commit to the hard seats of our economy-class cabin. It was that I wanted to find an island of personal space, that the train station was completely overwhelming. People with giant vinyl suitcases and cartons tied with string and tape. Boys rattling metal carriers stuffed with snacks and drinks. Big families sitting on mountains of possessions. Were they going somewhere, or did they live in the station? Women who had boldly thrown their burqas back over their heads—you could see their faces, the bright colors of their clothing showing underneath. Porters and hawkers and hucksters. Trains coming and going, debris and dust, the squeal of brakes, the unintelligible announcements over the public address system. The cars were green with yellow bars across the windows, close enough to keep a child from falling out, not so close as to keep you from buying a bag of salty mystery snacks from one of the station boys. Not so close as to keep you throwing from throwing candy wrappers and cigarette butts out the window as the train rolled through the countryside.

There were six seats to a compartment, and I was the only woman—again. I walked back to the women's car to take look. It was not as crowded, and the bathrooms were better, but I wanted to travel with Alastair. I was afraid to be alone for too long. In the world of men, I felt like a target if I was on my own. But next to Alastair, I was some weird kind of exotic pet, a talking dog, to whom the rules did not quite apply. It was okay for me to break all the conventions of their society under the auspices of my accompanying owner. In Alastair's presence, I was permitted to be my Western self, to look men directly in the eye, to ask questions, to be in the world with my legs bare from the knees down, my hair uncovered.

Four men occupied the other seats and they were excited to share space with us—their English was halting but sufficient for conversation. They shook Alastair's hand, nodded towards me, and smiled.

The train jerked its way out of the station, and I looked forward to an interesting journey.

The passing countryside was farms, homes made of mud bricks, the occasional mid-sized city with concrete buildings, apartments. We passed Mohenjo Daro, and I felt a twinge of regret that we were not getting off the train. The city is one of the world's oldest, the heart of the Indus River Valley. I remembered learning about it my high school anthropology classes, and there it was, out my window, a train station for the one of the oldest human-occupied places in the world. Why didn't we stop? There was no reason we could not have just gotten off the train to go exploring. But we acted like our journey toward the Indian border was on a schedule. We could not veer from our plan because . . . there was no good reason. The train pulled away and Mohenjo Daro was behind us, the cradle of human civilization just another dusty place, unreachable from the barred window of the train compartment.

The train rolled east towards the Indian border, and one of the men invited us to come home with him. Hamid was maybe thirty years old, maybe a bit younger, and he was on his way back to his village to meet the girl who would be his bride. A few days later, he would continue by car to Lahore, our destination. Did we want to come see where he lived?

I thought about the guy who had stopped and asked to show us around Karachi. About Eli's openness with strangers and how that made him so fun to travel with. About the driver who took us back to town when we walked back from the Coptic Church outside Cairo. I regretted missing Mohenjo Daro, not getting off the train, letting it disappear out the window. When was I going to be invited home to a rural Pakistani village, ever? Never, it was never going to happen again, so what the hell?

"What do you think?"

"He seems all right. I don't think he's going to kill us in our sleep," Alastair said.

Plus, it would cost us nothing, and we would end up in the right place, just a few days later.

It was late afternoon when we got off the train at Hamid's station and walked through the silent streets of a mud brick village. Hamid led us to a courtyard with a low building at the back, scrubby fields all around. A few open-fronted rooms faced into the walled patio, and that was it. Just beyond the wall there was a well, and we joined some children to wash in it. Hamid left us there for the night with some food and bottled water. He dragged two rough cots and out into the courtyard and gave us a pile of cotton blankets. We would sleep there for the night, and then he would fetch us the next day and bring us to his family.

The night was quiet, and when I sat up in the morning with the sunrise, a row of young children, boys and girls, were peeking over the wall looking at us. We could well have been the only foreign faces they had ever seen. We were, after all, on the edge of a rural village in the middle of Pakistan. I felt very far away in that moment, but fearless. Not that I wasn't afraid, but that there was nothing to worry about. We had slept well in the silence, and I had only woken up once, to a moonless sky full of stars.

Later that morning, Hamid took us to the small market in town and helped us buy better clothes for the region. He bought me a *shalwar kameez*—the baggy pants and long shirt the women wore under their burqas, and he insisted on buying a stack of shiny plastic bangles for my wrist. I was much more comfortable once dressed properly, not just for the climate but the culture too. I had a white and orange paisley patterned scarf that I kept over my head. Everything was lightweight cotton, pale colors. I was not hot, and everything was covered, so there was no modesty problem. Here in this country village women dressed this same way. They went about their lives, shopping and talking and living more openly than anywhere I'd been since leaving Israel.

Alastair was dressed in same local style—a pale green long shirt, baggy pants—and he looked like an Englishman gone native. I was grateful for my color, for my dark hair, for my green-brown eyes. My skin was lighter than most of the people around us. But compared to Alastair, so tall, so thin, his eyes so blue, I was almost invisible. I wasn't an immediate mark for something different. My eyes were too bold, I was too curious, but the clothes helped me feel less conspicuous, less likely to draw the ever-persistent harassment I'd experienced in Egypt.

Now we were properly dressed, Hamid was excited to take us places, to show us off. That night, we went to his bachelor party. At another farm, much like the place we'd spent the night, on the edge of the fields, a group of men lit a fire in an oil drum and four women danced to music from a portable tape player. The men waved faded currency at them and the women blushed and danced and tucked the notes into their pockets. I should not have been there, but I was again such a strange creature that it did not matter. The women were barefoot and dressed in bright colors. They wore jewelry on their faces, their wrists, around their necks. They touched the men on the arm, on the knee—Alastair too—and spun away laughing. It all seemed so harmless. I had seen more body contact at a junior high school dance, but I could tell that these women were not "good" women. They laughed loudly, they shimmied, they looked everyone directly in the eyes. The night darkened, the women danced in the light of the flames and at some point, when the fire had burned low, we got back in the car and Hamid returned us to his farm for the night.

Alastair had come down with a case of traveler's gut, quite a severe one. He was feverish and pale and could eat only plain rice. Hamid brought us to the house where his family lived and sent for the doctor. This house had a courtyard in back. You walked through the living room to a small garden with a tree in the middle, and the latrines to one side. His kids were out back, playing cards and tended to by his wife—wife number one. In the heat of the day we sprawled in the courtyard under the shade of the tree, while I read my Lonely Planet guide to India. The doctor appeared, a quiet man with a skullcap and beard, and he looked at us like we'd lost our minds.

"What are you people doing here in the middle of the countryside in the middle of the hot season?" he asked. He spoke perfect English, so his exasperation was perfectly clear.

It was a fair question. We'd come for a wedding celebration with a stranger we'd met on a train while heading to India from Karachi where we'd gone to get visas to India because, well, you could not cross Afghanistan right then because the mujahedeen were wandering around, armed by the Soviets.

That was not a good answer. How about we were here because Alastair's father wanted him to be a real estate agent and that wasn't going to happen. Plus, my mom was getting married again and my dad and my stepmom did not seem to care even the tiniest bit what I was doing with my life so we'd hooked up and headed east as though that was going to help us find out how to be adults. How about that?

Alastair shrugged. "We were invited."

The doctor fished some antibiotics from his old-fashioned doctor's bag. "You need to move on," he said. "You don't belong here."

It was hard to argue with him. We were taking much needed medication from his minimal supply. We didn't speak the language. We didn't understand the culture at all. We weren't there to help or work or do anything useful.

The doctor seemed satisfied when we told him we'd be off to India, that Hamid was taking us to the border in just two or three days. He gave Alastair instructions on how to take the medication, but his tone did not warm up. When they were done talking, he looked at us both again. He seemed angry, like our presence was an insult to him personally.

"You'll be leaving soon," he stated. It was not a question.

The next day, Hamid took us to meet his future bride. Men were allowed four wives, and this would be his second. We drove to another farm, crushed into the cab of Hamid's pickup truck and pulled up outside yet another mud brick building. A tree shaded a well out front, scrubby fallow fields surrounded us. We entered a small room; the door was a flap of fabric in the breeze. I sat down on the only piece of furniture, a string bed like the ones we'd slept on, next to a messy haired little girl with big eyes. She put her hand on my knee and we swung our feet together like it was a game. I kept expecting someone else to appear, but no one came. Hamid and Alastair stood outside just beyond the flap of cloth. Hamid waved his hand at the surrounding fields that would be his after the marriage, and then, they came back inside.

"My wife," Hamid said, gesturing towards the girl.

I felt sick and sad and completely powerless. I heard the doctor's question in my head again. "What are you people doing out here?"

That evening, back at the home where Hamid lived with his first wife, there was a large family dinner to celebrate the engagement. I stayed in the kitchen with the women, trying to have conversations, trying to help. In the back living room was an ancient uncle—over one hundred years old—and the women were eager to have me talk with him because he'd grown up speaking English. One of the women took me to a back room and sat me next to him on a scratchy horse-hair couch. He was so skinny, so small. He asked me questions about where I was from, where I was going. He had been in Pakistan before the partition with India—before it became its own country. He was envious of what he saw as Indian progress.

"Look at what they have done there," he said to me, "and think of what we have here. They understand progress." His effort to breathe out the words was audible. I sat patiently and listened. "You'll see what they've done after the partition," he said, "and look at us." He shook his head. Then, one of the women pulled me away to eat with the men while dinner was served. The women floated in and out of the dining room, refilling dishes of rice and curry, topping up glasses of tea.

Late that night, we piled into the back of a pickup truck and made for Lahore. Two of Hamid's friends were coming too. They had the cab of the truck; we had piled blankets and pillows in the bed. I tried to sleep but the bounce of the truck bed was constant, and either Hamid's hands were wandering or I was dreaming they were. I woke up Alastair and asked him to switch places with me. For the rest of the night I watched the sky roll by overhead, pinned between Alastair and the wheel well of the pickup bed.

In the morning, we arrived in Lahore and stopped at the Bashari Mosque, all red sandstone and elaborate inlay work. I did not know what there was to see in Lahore. Like so many places we went, this was just a stop on the way to somewhere else, an unexpected place for which I had no context. But the mosque was beautiful. Even in my ignorance, I could see what a magnificent building it was. Shiny bits of bright turquoise and dark blue and emerald green stones were set in painstaking mosaics everywhere. We climbed up to the ramparts and looked out over the walled city of Lahore.

A group of schoolboys approached behind us, chattering, swirling. They were twelve, maybe fourteen years old, tops. I was standing at the edge of the wall watching groups of women in blue burqas walk past the shops on the streets below. One of the boys grabbed my ass and laughed.

I turned around and punched him on the shoulder, not hard, just enough to make him step back. Then I pushed him away, right below his solar plexus. He bumped into the boy behind him, stunned, and everyone gasped. I did too. What had I just done?

I was so tired. I stood in the heat and the stillness of this terrible moment, completely worn down.

"Miss, I am so sorry," I looked around to see where the voice was coming from. "They never see women like you out in public." He was their teacher. They were on a class field trip to see the mosque. He turned to the boy who had grabbed me. "He will apologize," he said to me, and then said turned to the boy and said something I could not understand.

The boy looked at his feet and put his hands in a prayer position. He nodded a small nod. He did, indeed, look contrite. He said something and nodded again.

The teacher spoke him in a serious voice before turning to look at me again. "I am so sorry," he said, one more time. I nodded sideways, not a yes or a no, and I gave him a half smile.

It seemed impossible to get anything done in one of those burqas. But no one would see you. You would be a drape of cloth, nothing more. I had seen so few women in Karachi. In the countryside, they were out in the open, dressed like I now was in a *shalwar kameez*, maybe a scarf thrown over their heads. But you could see their faces. Here in Lahore, women were out in public, but you could not see them at all.

It was fundamentalists. These extremists—they would later become the Taliban—had spilled over from Afghanistan into Northeastern Pakistan. They were powerful here, and they required women to be completely covered. The apology helped, the teacher's kind voice helped, but I felt a twist of fear, a sharpness that went beyond the usual street corner annoyances that were part of being a woman in parts of the world where women didn't look or act like I did. This was different.

"They never see women like you," he had said.

For the first time, I wondered why that was. In that moment I realized I might be in danger. I had not seen one Western woman traveling since we'd left Cairo. Alastair had not learned he needed to watch me, to act as though I was his. I wanted him to be a barrier between me and the men who looked at me like a circus animal, but he simply did not notice. I was lucky that this teacher was kind. A different man, a different kind of teacher, things could have gone in a different direction. I was glad to be near the Indian border. I was eager to get out of Pakistan.

Hamid drove us to hotel in the old city, a small place up a few flights of stairs. The room looked out over busy streets full of burqa clad women wandering the sidewalks in groups of two or three, never alone. Alastair had got it in his head that Hamid was going to pay for the room, and when Hamid refused Alastair began to shout at him. The hotel lobby filled with his voice. "You said you would pay," Alastair yelled. Hamid's face was a mixture of confusion and embarrassment. The money was nothing. It could not have been ten dollars for the night, less, probably. But Alastair was in a rage. I knew I would wear his anger on my arms later, so I said nothing.

Hamid had taken us off from train to his family, to his home. He'd fed us, taken care of us, and called the doctor for Alastair when he was sick. Then, he delivered us to Lahore just as he had promised. I wore the stack of bangles he'd bought me on my right wrist. He refused to take money for anything. He acted insulted when I tried to pay him for the clothes he'd bought us. His generosity was sincere.

Hamid was also about to marry a child, a girl who could not have been more than eight years old. This scene in the hotel lobby made me angry. I was angry at feeling so ignorant about where I was, angry at how powerless I felt. And I was embarrassed. I could not believe Alastair was yelling at the man who had shown us nothing but kindness. He was being an asshole about a ten-dollar hotel room. I picked up the room key from the counter, walked down the hall, and closed the door behind me.

In the morning when we checked out, I paid the bill.

CHAPTER SEVENTEEN:
The Hill Towns

The train was rumbling on the tracks, going nowhere. I was back in my Western clothes, feeling lighter and a little bit bored, walking the length of platform. Alastair stood in the shadow of the station, out of the hot sun. We had already cleared immigration—a rubber-stamp process, what with our India visas sorted back in Karachi. But it was a border checkpoint, and everyone had to be admitted. We had to wait until the entire train was cleared to enter India. I paced back and forth, back and forth, watching the immigration police go in and out of the rail cars, watching the passengers duck in and out of the customs office, listening to the hum of the train engine.

I was tired of sitting. The ride had not been all that long, but it was good to move again after feeling so folded into myself those last days in Pakistan. After I passed the engine the third or fourth time, the conductor stepped out and said hello.

"I love trains," I said. "I love traveling by train."

The conductor was handsome and bearded and wore a pale blue turban. "Do you want to see how the engine gets fed?" I leaned into the heat of the cabin. He opened a heavy metal gate to show me where the coal turned to motion.

There were two men working the engine, calm in their coal-dusted clothes, black soot around their eyes and noses, easy and friendly in their manner. I waved to Alastair to come join me; we both accepted the invitation to step into the resting machine, to see the levers and feel the heat. One of the engineers mixed up glasses of peppery lime-ade—the ingredients pulled from a cabinet behind the coal box—and handed them to us. "The pepper keeps you cool on these hot days," he said.

I did not like the taste and it did not help break the heat at all, but I liked that I'd been offered it, and I drank it graciously. I liked these two men with dirty faces, their cheerful attitudes. I especially liked that I felt like myself again for the first time in much too long. It felt like it might be easier on the Indian side of the border. I was no longer locked out by a language barrier, and there were women everywhere, living their lives, right out in the open.

When the train finally set in motion again, two drop-dead hand-some guys with the darkest skin I had ever seen joined us. They were students from Nairobi. Alastair and the guys set off on a lively conver-sation, but I could not understand a word they said. It was my fault, not theirs; I could not tune my ear to their Kenyan-accented English. They could see this, these guys, by the way I looked at them every time they addressed me directly. Once, one of them laughed and said, right out, "You don't understand a word I'm saying, do you?" I blushed; I was embarrassed, and I apologized.

We got off the train in Amritsar and headed to a hotel listed in my guidebook. The streets were full of uncovered women going about their business. There was not a burqa in sight. The men wore turbans and younger boys had their hair up in topknots covered in cloth. Many of the women were dressed like I'd been in Pakistan, covered from the sun, but you could see their faces. If they were wearing saris, you could see their bellies, their arms. The city was bright and busy. A cow wandered across an intersection. Bicycle rickshaws swirled around us. Much of the signage was in English and it felt like a layer of confusion had been peeled off simply by crossing the border. Understanding was now about accents more than vocabulary. I only had to adjust my internal antennae until I'd found the right frequency. We ran into one of the guys from Nairobi a few days later and it turned out I could understand him just fine. I apologized to him again, and he laughed.

"I'm glad to see you," he said, before asking Alastair for money. Did he think we were so rich that we would give money to a random guy we'd met on the train forty-eight hours before? I suppose we could have been. How would he know? We were knocking around without jobs or purpose, so maybe it wasn't a bad assessment.

"Sorry, man," Alastair said, and the Kenyan guy wandered off in the opposite direction.

Our room had a TV and a big swamp cooler that stuck out of the window facing onto the second-floor walkway. Breakfast was included, along with endless cups of tea supplied in the hotel lobby. The swamp cooler did not work at first, and it was necessary in the oppressive Punjabi heat. I fetched the receptionist from the front desk, and he gave the reluctant machine a solid whack on the side, after which it hummed into life, blowing wet breath into the room. I lay on the bed staring at the ceiling, at the light cast through the louvered windows, watching the news in Hindi on a static prone TV. I flipped through my guidebook. It was a year out of date, but it had got us to this hotel room, had told us how to get Indian currency. It issued appropriately alarmist warnings about the spiciness of local food—much spicier than you could ever imagine. Really. You should not try to show off by pretending that you knew from and liked spicy food because you had no idea.

Alastair had wanted to come to India because the word from travelers—from the day he left England—was that you could live there forever for cheap, and quite well too. If you had some savings, it would take you ages to run them down. You could see the country. You could hang out somewhere you liked, maybe live outdoors if you were in a region where the weather was mild enough. People said it was safe. Your biggest worry was getting pick-pocketed, and that could happen in Tel Aviv, after all. You could pick up some intestinal virus—and you probably would—but we'd been through that in Pakistan. It could be cured. India was a place where you could do nothing for a long time, with no pressure from anyone to be successful or useful or anything at all. As long as you had enough money—and it was not all that much—to feed and house yourself, you'd be fine.

I had wanted to come to India because of all my reading. Kipling, Orwell, Forster's *Passage to India*, Theroux's *Great Railway Bazaar*, which I'd read over and over. India seemed like a dream. Not like the fulfillment of some ambition or some idealistic view of things. Not like the romance of Paris. Not that kind of dream at all.

It's one thing to hear stories about cows being sacred and to understand that you might see them in the street. It's another to see one in the middle of a whirling intersection, surrounded by rickshaws and bicycles and the occasional taxi or private car. A large white cow in the center of a hurricane of urban motion, walking as though she has a specific destination in mind, does not quite make sense. It was that kind of dream, an *Alice in Wonderland* kind of dream. If the cow had turned and asked what I was staring at, it would have been consistent with everything happening around me. I'd seen so much, but to still be surprised and overwhelmed by the strangeness of every day in India made me feel like I was a little bit high all the time. The sharpness of the light, the noise, the brightness of the colors, the spicy flavors of the food. Everything felt like it was more of itself, like the saturation had been turned up, along with the volume. It was like a dream where nothing made sense, but there it was. You took it at face value because it was happening right in front of you.

I had wanted to go into the mountains, to touch the sky draped across the highest peaks in the world. This ambition did not make sense for me. I liked camping but I hated backpacking. I was still strong from farm work, but I was not built to carry a pack. When I was twelve or thirteen, I'd gone on a two-week backpacking trip in the Sierra Nevada mountains with a YMCA youth group. I was the smallest of the girls. There was one boy, who was smaller than me, but people liked him. He was cute and funny; he had mascot potential. I was not cute. I was awkward and bony and weak. I was often the last to reach camp at night. I struggled to keep pace and every morning when I woke up, I was disappointed to find the trip was not over. That small boy in our group was applauded every evening when he arrived at camp, but I was given no pity, no congratulations for making the same effort. It's a wonder I still loved the outdoors. But even on that trip, which was so hard, I had embraced the blue of the sky at altitude, the clarity of the air when you got above the trees. I was enchanted by the idea that people lived so close to the sky, and I wanted to go up as far as I could manage.

I was not in a hurry, it seemed like there was nothing but time. We could figure things out at our leisure and then decide what route we wanted to take. We knew if we wanted to cross the mountains we must do so before winter, but beyond that it seemed we were in an endless summer, that the orange heat of the sky would last as long as we needed it to.

We hung out in Amritsar for a few days, trying to find a place to eat where the food was not too spicy for our soft Western palates. The first few times Alastair and I walked away from half-eaten meals, inedible because of their fire. It wasn't until after we learned to temper the heat with yogurt that it became possible to get through a full dinner. We wandered town looking for things to do, roaming the market, reading local English-language newspapers and not understanding the relevance of what we were reading at all.

We stood in line to visit the Golden Temple, studying the large hand-lettered signs that explained who the Sikh people were. This was their home country, the temple their Jerusalem. Inside the temple, I tossed marigolds on to the dais where a bearded man sat surrounded by flowers, quietly praying. It's what others were doing, so I did too. We exchanged our cash pounds and dollars for rupees after following men we met on the steps of the bank into back alleys, tucking the stacks of brightly colored bills into bags we wore around our necks. Back in the hotel we watched soap operas and the news in Hindi on the television and read newspapers that had been discarded in the lobby.

Alastair was still recovering from the bad gut he'd got in Pakistan and I was just so fucking tired from the grind of Egypt, of Pakistan. It was nice to stop in this place where I could go outside without it being an incident. Beyond the door of the hotel, there were so many inconsistent things happening all at once, and once we'd crossed the border, I was just one more, Alastair was just one more. We weren't worthy even of notice. That was a relief. We'd see other Western travelers now and then, other pale faces, bodies in Western dress. We were no longer the only ones. I was content to be written off as another lost hippie. It was such a relief to just be ignored.

I'd read about how Rudyard Kipling had lived in Shimla. According to my guidebook, you could get to Shimla via a narrow-gauge railway that was pretty and fun. We had seen the Golden Temple, the significant sight in Amritsar, taken a few days to become as grounded as we would ever be, and I was bored with television. After repeatedly asking the front desk clerk to smack the swamp cooler, I had figured it out myself. I did not want to be in a relationship with this swamp cooler, and there was no apparent reason for us to stay in town. We booked overnight tickets to Chandigarh where we would change trains and ride the rest of the way to Shimla on that picturesque little railway.

It was impossible to get a decent night's sleep on the train. It was not the train itself. It was easy to get used to the sound and the motion, the steady rock of the car, the song of the wheels. But the stations— the stations blasted chaos into the rhythm of the ride. It did not matter if it was the middle of the night when the train rolled into a station; the cars were beset upon with boys with metal trays and glasses of milky tea. They'd rattle the windows with sticks, waking you out of whatever sleep you'd fallen into, then wave their hands around, fists full of plastic bags of snacks. "Chai, memsahib," they'd say, "snacks, sahib." I'd hang my head over the top bunk and look out the window at the yellowy light of the platform. People were stretched out on sheets of cardboard on the ground, their shoes a pillow. Others scrambled to get on or off during the shorter stops. I'd drift off as the train pulled away from the station into the darkened landscape, only to go through the whole thing all over again at the next station. The whistle as we arrived, the rush of activity, the boys shouting to sell things from the platform and then, again, the rocking motion of the train in the nighttime.

Shimla was once a retreat for British colonists trying to escape the heat of the lower plains. The air in Shimla was misty and cool. The terraced hillsides were checkered with elaborate houses. Some were timbered as though the British had decided Shimla was their alpine village, a mash-up of India and Switzerland all at once.

The town was also was overrun with monkeys. Monkeys sat on the stone walls that lined the main promenade, they lurked in doorways, they threw things at the train. They were nasty, dangerous creatures and you did not want anything to do with them. We spent a few days wandering, avoiding the monkeys, cooling off in the mountain air, and then headed back down to Chandigarh via the same pretty, narrow-gauge train.

Alastair was increasingly a liability. The Indians we met did not want to talk to him. The guesthouses had no rooms when he asked. He could not hail a rickshaw; he could not negotiate for better prices in the markets. People we encountered were perfectly willing to engage me in whatever theater was required to do business, but they had no time for my tall English companion.

I would leave Alastair with our bags on the sidewalk. Then I'd go into whatever hotel we'd chosen, get a room, and return with Alastair once the deal was sorted. I always told the desk clerk that my boyfriend was with the bags and please, could I see the room first? It was "No problem, Miss," and "Of course, memsahib." Always. I loved the formal language of these transactions. But Alastair's experience was different. He would always get "Sorry, full up."

I did not take joy in this, partly because it angered Alastair, partly because it was tiring to be the voice for our travels. But it was the only way to move forward. I could not figure out why the Indians, always approachable and kind to me, disliked him on sight. I began to wonder if they saw something immediately that I did not see, or if it was as simple as history. He was English, the historic perpetrator of colonial crimes. I was small and dark-haired, but by no stretch of the imagination could I pass as local. Nor was I attempting to do so, but I didn't encounter the resistance he experienced every time he opened his mouth.

It was a relief to be back in a place where women were part of the environment again. India's inequality was present in every single moment of every day. But compared to Egypt, where it seemed there were only two kinds of women in public, wives and grandmothers, or Pakistan, where women were ghosts in blue, women in India participated in society. It was no Israel, where you were just as likely to sit next to a young woman in full military fatigues and carrying a machine gun as you were likely to sit next to a young man doing the same. But women were present, active. I felt better traveling in India than I'd felt anywhere for months. Better, even, than I'd felt in Israel where the boys were so aggressive with their attentions that sometimes, it was easier to not go out than it was to go out alone. When we stopped in Chandigarh, I stood on the platform listening to the train idle, watching people coming and going, and I felt more solid than I'd ever felt.

As long as we were headed towards the mountains, I was content. I was going to cross the Himalayas, one way or another, and I would take my time getting there. Alastair was healthy again, the weather in the foothills was cool and getting around was so cheap. Meals were cheap, beds were cheap. Transportation was cheap. We wound our way north, navigating the chaos of local buses, trusting that when the crew tossed our bags up on to the roof, we would get them back again—and we did. Sometimes local people stared, but sometimes they started conversations, gave advice about where to go, asked questions, answered ours. The sensory input was consistently over-whelming, but even with that, being in India was easier than where we'd been.

We worked our way up to Srinagar where the shores of Lake Dal were lined with houseboats. A traveler could book a room on the water with three meals a day for a few dollars. The houseboats were long and low and had elaborately carved balconies and shutters. They had out-house-sized bathrooms, shared living-room-like spaces draped in car-pets, and more elaborately carved furniture. Srinagar was not just a place where backpackers landed, though they were a common sight. Indian families came here too. The Indian people we talked to in shops and restaurants were often tourists just like we were, regular middle-class people who also wanted to feel the mountain air. Alastair would have denied our similarity. We could not just be tourists—you had to be on vacation for that. You had to be a working stiff with a job to have a vacation from. We thought ourselves better than that, for reasons I would not have been able to explain.

During the day, if it was not raining, we would wander the city looking at the jade and cashmere that visitors who liked to shop spent their money on. In one jewelry store, I asked the clerk to tell me how you know the jade is real, and he took a lighter to a bracelet, waited until it was covered with soot, and wiped it clean. The markets were lined with stalls selling soft Kashmiri shawls and scratchy sweaters, the wool so rough and full of lanolin that it kept the rain out. I bought an off-white sweater knitted with an abstract pattern around the middle and wore it at night to keep the chill off after the sun set.

The houseboat was run by two young men who were about my age, maybe a year or two older. They were talkers, and genuinely friendly. In the mornings there was tea and flatbread, sometimes eggs, in the evenings a full meal, rice and curry, sometimes with chicken, but mostly vegetarian. Every now and then, after dinner we'd get high with the other guests. In the evenings, I'd spend what was left of the daylight staring over the water while the sky turned to dark blue and then to black, twinkling lights from the houseboats reflecting on the water of the lake. In the mornings, the sun would warm the air and I would peek out from under a pile of blankets to see a ball of orange in the sky, trying to burn through the mist, reflected on the surface of the still lake.

The lake had little gondolas strung with marigolds and one day we took one because it was what you did here, even though we were on the water all the time. The gondolier took us out on to the middle of the water and looking back, you could see the city creeping up the foothills to the north and disappearing into the clouds. You could see all the lake-facing market stalls and the little houseboats, everywhere, not just for tourists, but also, for families that lived on the shores of the lake. I wasn't supposed to like this kind of activity, but it was fun to embrace being a tourist, and so easy to do in this town that was full of tourists anyway. Here it was less and less unusual to see Western travelers—a white girl in a sari over there, an English boy who had twisted his hair into dreadlocks at her side, Germans, always in their leather pants no matter what the weather was.

We stayed in Srinagar for a week and then, restless, decided to head to higher altitudes. Another mountain town would be our gateway for a weeklong walk across a low but manageable pass. We'd try this as a test run for a longer trek. We took a bus to a river town in the mist-draped forests below a mountainous national park. The town was stuck along a ridge on one side of the river, and spread to the opposite bank. A trail led into the forest and out into a broad meadow at the edge of a national park. After half a day's walk we came to a village where there were cabins for park visitors—little houses, really—maintained and serviced by a family living nearby. One of the rooms was taken by a pair of German guys who intended to cross the same pass we wanted to walk over. We hung out for two nights, making plans for the walk, but I'd gotten sick. Weak from a bad cold, I spent most of the time in bed, drinking tea.

Alastair was committed to the trek, but, as sick as I was, there was no way I was going to make it. We decided to part ways. We'd meet again in Srinagar. Hopefully we'd be able to get back on the same houseboat where we'd stayed before. If nothing else, I'd leave a message there as to where I was staying. Alastair set out across the meadow and I turned back into the forest, walking the first few miles back to town on my own. Halfway through the day, a pair of Australian girls appeared behind me, amazed to find me walking alone. They asked me how I ended up out there solo, and I told them what had happened. "Aren't you afraid?" they asked. It hadn't crossed my mind that I should be.

The three of us walked together to a guest house on the far side of the river, back at the trailhead. It was an immaculate little inn with a dining room. I booked a snug wood paneled bedroom with two high single beds piled deep with blankets, and a view across the river into town. I had a room to myself for the first night. The next day the desk clerk asked if he could put another American in my room with me. I said it was no bother, as long as he did not keep me from my sleep.

He was a nice guy from Philadelphia, traveling alone. He'd come a similar route to mine, first in Israel, then India, though not via Pakistan as I had. I genuinely enjoyed the company. I did not mind having a roommate, and it did not occur to me to be bothered that I had to share my room. My bed was on the side with the window. Every morning I let the cool air of the forest in while I looked across at clouds that seemed to be below the level of the inn. I'd stay in bed until I smelled breakfast cooking. Then I'd pad down the hall in my stocking feet to the dining room. I'd join the other travelers and we'd trade stories and travel advice over chai and fried eggs and naan.

I rarely left the guest house, staying either in the dining room or perched on my high bunk. One morning I wandered across the river into town to go to a pharmacy—my cold had turned into a sinus infection. While waiting for the antibiotics to kick in I read my guide-book and made plans for heading even further north. The rest of the time I spent looking out the window, sleeping, and drinking tea in bed.

The inn was small; maybe it had a dozen rooms. One of the guests was from Belgium. He was taking sitar lessons. During the afternoons and evenings, the sound of his practicing would wander down the stairs and under the door of my room. It was a perfect place to regain my health. My roommate was quiet and kind, the air smelled like pine trees and mountain snow, and there was a live soundtrack from the sitar down the hall. I was happy to rest in bed, to drink tea, to trade stories with the other guests.

I stayed until I felt well enough to take the bus back to Srinagar. I hurled my bag into the rack over the seat and settled in for the ride. The man in front of me turned around to look at me with an open face. "Excuse me, Miss," he said, gently, "Can I ask you a question?"

"Of course, of course." India had made me less defensive in conversation than I'd been for a long time. The people I met genuinely wanted to talk. And without Alastair's Britishness—or whatever it was about him as an obstacle—conversations were easy and frequent.

"It's about the food in your country."

I laughed. My fellow bus passenger had lived in the United States for a while and confessed that he had found American food completely tasteless. "No flavor," he said. "None at all. Is it . . . supposed to be like that?"

I laughed some more. "You know, it took me a while before I could eat the food here," I said. "Everything was so spicy at first. It's better now, but when I first got to India, I could not eat anything but yogurt without feeling like the skin on my tongue was burning off."

The bus rattled back into town and I went to the houseboat where we'd stayed before, where there was still a room open. Two nights later, Alastair appeared, worn from the trip but fine.

"The pass was covered with snow," he told me, "and we were up to our hips in the stuff. I thought we would never get across." He was in good spirits, if tired, and I was envious that he'd been up above the tree line. But I knew I'd made the right choice. If the snow was deep on him—he was over six feet tall—I would not have been able to make it through. He told me that the nights had been very cold, and they had seen no other people. He was eager to go further into the mountains and, healed after plenty of rest, I was too. I was excited to walk up into the sky.

I had liked the time I'd spent alone though. It was so much easier than traveling with Alastair. No one hurt me, ever. I had people to talk to, strangers were kind to me, and the logistics—the business of finding a room, getting a bus ticket, sitting down to a meal—felt so much lighter when I was on my own. I felt stronger alone than I did when I was in Alastair's company.

But not once did I consider changing my plans, leaving him wondering where I had gone and if he would ever see me again. There was never any question in my mind that I would meet him back at the lake in Srinagar, never any doubt that we would continue our travels together. I had walked through the forest alone, spent a few days talking care of myself, and found my way back to the city. It was clear I was completely capable of managing on my own. I'd been managing most of the transactional parts of our travel since we'd crossed into India. I didn't need Alastair at all. I'd have been better off without him, but I followed the plan as though it was unchangeable, as though there was no other choice. The women I met on the trail saw me as some kind of fierce solo traveler, but I was trapped in Alastair's vision of a smaller, weaker, worthless person. I couldn't see anything else. I couldn't see myself without him.

CHAPTER EIGHTEEN:
To Touch the Sky

As we traveled north into Ladakh, the roads were choked with military vehicles. Great convoys of trucks crawled up the narrow, winding roads towards the border between India and China. People we met spoke of the continuing dispute between the two countries.

Our bus inched along behind olive green army vehicles, behind supply trucks full of farming goods and other merchandise, pulling on to the narrow shoulder whenever a vehicle needed to squeeze pass in the other direction. We were heading to Leh, high in the mountains. The trip was tedious, with long hours grinding up graded dirt roads. The hours were punctuated by occasional moments in which my life flashed before my eyes as the bus tilted over the edge of gravelly canyons. The rivers were so far below they looked no wider than a string of silver wire.

Every now and then there'd be a village clinging to the slope above the road. The bus would stop at a little café or roadside turnout with a tea stall. Passengers would spill out to buy glasses of hot tea with milk, maybe a plate of lentil curry with rice, maybe a candy bar. We'd stand in the sunshine, grateful to feel the ground under our feet, so reassuring after the dizzying lean of the bus. Mountains appeared and disappeared on the horizon. There were always more, and when the sky lifted, it revealed more mountains, always higher than the row in front of them.

Once I looked across a roadside gulch at a giant bodhisattva carved from the face of a rock cliff. He seemed a thousand years old, and his face was serene as he watched over all of us, tourists and soldiers and farmers, while we ate curry and roadside snacks. As I stood studying the monumental sculpture, a man walked over to me and addressed me in Hindi. I laughed because of course I did not speak Hindi, then he laughed when I told him where I was from. "You could be from Northern India," he said, gesturing toward my hair. "Your color . . . " he trailed off.

It was still summer. The snow was as melted as it was going to be, the skies were a fully saturated blue, and the air was warm during the day. When we arrived in Leh, we got a room at a mud brick guest house and I spent the first few days bolting back and forth from our room to the outhouse with a wicked case of traveler's gut. It got so the young women who ran the place would get out of the way if they saw me coming. After three days of this, I went to the local clinic where I tested positive for giardia and salmonella—two common diseases carried by bad food and bad water. It took a few days for me to feel better after I started medication. But I had started to drop weight like crazy because no matter what I ate, it would not stay in my gut long enough to fuel me. I was not alone; there was always someone in the common area of the guest house nursing a cup of tea and a dish of plain rice, waiting for the meds to kick in and for their guts to settle.

This is what travelers did in Leh. They waited for their guts to settle. They inventoried their gear for the trek over the Taglang La Pass down into the lower foothills and plains to the south. They waited for the runs to the outhouse to become less frequent. They stopped for a few days to adjust to the altitude before climbing farther up into the sky.

The travelers we met were either serious mountaineers or rough-edged road junkies. The mountain climbers had more money, better gear, and return tickets. The road junkies had an attitude that would probably look like addiction in their home countries. We were all skinny, our clothes worn thin, bits of local attire layered on top of whatever we'd been wearing when we set out. My yak-wool sweater, a string of beads tied around some guy's wrist, a gorgeous shawl tied around a girl's waist like a skirt.

Leh was also a center for Tibetan Buddhist refugees and there was a palace here, a smaller version of the Tibetan capital in Lhasa. There were a lot of Buddhist temples and retreats in and around Leh. They'd been there for centuries. We visited the monasteries and counted thousands of frescoed Buddhas, left whatever odd things we had in our pockets on the altars, and hung out with other travelers in places that had dumplings and beer. We traded stories about how we'd got there, where we'd been. But because being there was a badge in itself, there was no need competition.

One afternoon the whole town spilled down the road to the monastery courtyard for an annual festival celebrating the birthday of a Tibetan Buddhist master. We watched monks blow long brass horns and play drums. I followed Alastair, unmistakable at a full head taller than nearly everyone around. We sat on the hard ground shoulder to shoulder with local people and a handful of tourists. There were dancers in masks and brightly embroidered robes. We watched monks

blow long brass horns and play drums. There was a lot of deep chant-
ing, rumbling noises I could feel behind my sternum while I sat on the
concrete in the sun. It was beautiful and scary at the same time. There
were so many death heads decorating the masks, and fierce red demon
faces, and the bright blue of the mountain sky like a backdrop behind
all of it.

I liked this part of the country. I liked the pace and the easygoing
vibe, and I liked the magic of dropping in and out of the monasteries,
the monks—and sometimes nuns—so quiet and calm. I imagined
myself in some kind of smaller Tibet, a smaller Lhasa, and I was not
entirely wrong. The white palace at the top of the city was in the
Tibetan style, and there were so many Tibetans here, refugees from
China's occupation of their home country. This part of the Himalayas
was Tibetan Buddhist long before European or Chinese colonists
redrew the map, long before India and China argued over which part
of the mountains were theirs.

In town, there were shops where girls wove complicated beautiful
rugs. In other shops, boys made prayer scrolls, intricate paintings in
bright primary colors, bodhisattvas holding a different object, each
with meaning, in their hundreds of delicate hands. The local people
greeted us gently, welcomed us in to watch them making art, and
sometimes asked if we wanted to take pictures. It was quiet because
there were so few vehicles and power was intermittent. When the grid
was up, you'd hear Bob Marley or Eric Clapton spilling out of a
boom-box in a café, cassette tapes left behind by previous backpackers. Occasionally you'd hear the engine of a cargo truck that had
arrived full of goods and a new tumble of hitchhikers would appear.
But mostly, it was wind and quiet voices and sometimes, laughter. I
felt good here, close to the sky.

My gut finally settled enough to move on. Like the other travelers, we inventoried our gear. A tent, two sleeping bags. A heavy brass stove with a single burner and small fuel tank. I had a raincoat and my sweater, a set of rough long underwear, a pair of sneakers. Bags of rice and dried chickpeas. My camera and a few rolls of film. My 1981 *Lonely Planet India* guidebook. Not nearly enough gear, and not the right kind to make a two-week journey on foot across the towering pass. We were very poorly prepared. We went anyway.

After Leh, there were no more buses; it was the end of the line for public transportation. We had to hitchhike. But it was easy to get a ride—if a truck went by, it stopped. The military could not—or would not—pick us up, but the regular truck drivers picked up everyone, backpackers and local people alike. We went from tiny mountain village to tiny mountain village, sometimes in the cab, sometimes in the bed with locals perched on whatever cargo the truck was carrying. The rides were short, stops were frequent, but I did not mind because it was always interesting.

On the first day hitchhiking, we ran out of daylight and traffic stopped. Of course, no one was driving these treacherous mountain roads in the dark. We found a glade of trees and made camp. In the morning, a solider shook our tent to wake us before asking us how we'd ended up there. We had somehow crossed on to a military base and had pitched the tent not far from the barracks. The nights were so dark; we could not see the buildings. Maybe they had no power that evening—generators out, wires out, who knows. We were not supposed to be there, but the soldier was more embarrassed by finding us than we were by being found. He did not rush us while we packed up, and he wished us luck as he pointed us back down towards the road where we would pick up our next ride.

After a long day of hitchhiking, we ended up at another monastery festival drinking *chhaang*, a kind of Tibetan beer made by local people. The tangy brew was scooped out of a giant plastic bucket with a plastic mug and passed hand to hand. The celebrating locals called us into their circle and insisted we drink too. The Ladakhi people were wrapped in coral and turquoise jewelry, the women wore elaborate winged headdresses. We could not converse, but it did not matter, no one seemed to care as long as there was plenty to drink. Shortly before sunset and quite drunk, we staggered into the meadow below the monastery to pitch the tent. We woke up to a delegation of women and children encircling our portable nylon home. We'd been told that they would ask us for medication, for first aid-kit kind of stuff, and they did, but we had nothing to give them. We broke camp while the women and children watched, then wandered back across the meadow to the road to hitch another ride.

On the last day of hitching, we camped with three Americans who were supporting a climbing party up on a peak that disappeared into the sky above us. The Americans had been there for a few days waiting for the climbers to come back down. We pitched our tent a polite distance away and joined the Americans to smoke weed and get very, very high. We laughed ourselves silly as marmots appeared, late in the afternoon, making the meadow appear like a giant game of whack-a-mole.

Again, in the morning, there was a delegation of women and children—it was not apparent where they'd come from—and again we disappointed them by not having medical supplies to give them. Again we knew what they were asking for because we'd been told by other travelers. They asked, we said no, and we went on to eyeing each other with open curiosity. It was all so easy going. It's not that they didn't want anything. But they didn't expect it, and there was no noticeable change in attitude when we shrugged and signed that we had nothing to give.

At this very last stretch of road, the drivers stopped anytime there was someone on the roadside. Everyone moved over so new passengers could wedge in, crushed against a shipment of lumber, or bags of rice, or boxes of construction materials, or whatever. That was how we arrived in Kargil, crushed into the bed of a truck with two dozen locals, all of us coated in road dust, all of us huddled down low against the wind. Battered by the road, shoulder to shoulder with Tibetans, Ladhakis. And there we were, two Westerners, Alastair towering over the local people, but just as red-cheeked and road worn as everyone else.

It was hard work to get to Kargil—the long trips over rough roads, the hours perched on top of cargo in the back of trucks, the roadside camping at night—so it was good to take a rest before whatever was going to come next. Instead of pressing on immediately for higher altitudes, we took a break from the slog of transit for a few days to wander around the timbered village. Alastair and I spent the first night in a guest house and I woke up covered in welts. Bedbugs were rampant, and I'd been eaten alive all night. We moved to another place the next night after a local in a restaurant noticed my bite-covered arms. He gave me the name of a place he promised was clean, and when we checked in, the receptionist shook his head at the red spots covering my skin. "Terrible," he said. "Those places are terrible. I promise you, no bites here."

The faces on the local people had changed with gain in altitude. They were rounder with almond-shaped eyes, and they weren't as brown as they were where we'd come from, first in Amritsar, and then in Srinagar. Kids were everywhere, boys and girls, hanging out in shop doorways, playing in the streets, smiling and sweet with their wind chapped cheeks. Everyone was dressed in thick, wooly sweaters, dark brown or maroon, and knitted caps. Everyone looked bright-eyed and curious. It was fun to wander this rabbit warren of a town with no destination in mind, drinking beer and eating yak meat dumplings and slurping warm cups of butter tea. The salty broth-like drink acted like a jumpstart on cold mornings and served as good fuel as the air grew thinner.

The lower reaches of the mountains were covered in terraced farms, bright green paddies, stucco and timber houses, two and three stories tall. There were almost no cars, just military trucks and cargo. The mornings were so cold it was hard to crawl out of bed, but once the sun had cleared the mountains, it was good to be outside. The light was hard and bright, and the colors seemed richer in the clear air. It felt like you could see forever.

The weather was good and was forecast to stay dry for a while. I was healthy again. Or healthy enough—I had lost a great deal of weight. Any muscle I had left from farm work was now tight to my bones. I was stringy and sharp. But I felt fine, up for adventure, and if we were going to do the week-long trek, over the Taglang La Pass, it was time to go.

We'd chosen this walk because it was the most accessible, the least technical. We might have to wade across some shallow rivers, but there were no steep glacier crossings, and we would not need special equipment. According to my guidebook the trail was well marked. My guidebook recommended booking Sherpas to help carry your gear. The altitude could be challenging, but a sturdy walker with basic backpacking gear could complete this route with little trouble, especially if the weather cooperated.

We considered ourselves prepared enough. We shouldered our bags and headed uphill. The dirt road narrowed over the course of the day until it was nothing more than a narrow well-beaten horse path. There were white stucco *stupas*—trailside shrines—along the route, strings of prayer flags and prayer stones. Way finding was easy. But Alastair's bag was heavy and mine was just wrong for backpacking. The stove had a leak and was dripping white gas on to Alastair's limited belongings. He stopped to tie it on the outside of his bag, and we continued. The walking was hard because we were so high up. We'd been at altitude for at least a week, and still, the simple work of walking while carrying a load was exhausting. We stopped frequently to drink water and rest. We were surprised to make the first campsite well before sunset.

Another party was setting up camp in the meadow. They'd hired Sherpas in Kargil, two young men with four sturdy round ponies. That's what we should have done. We should have hired Sherpas with ponies to help carry the gear. We were always doing things the hard way because Alastair didn't want to spend money. He was constantly worried about the money running out. He'd take supreme discomfort or bad choices over spending a few more dollars. He acted like there would never be a way to get more money, and what we had was all we would ever have. It would have been smart to join a trekking party before leaving town, but Alastair decided we could do this on our own. I didn't want to fight him on it. In a rare moment of common sense, he admitted he was wrong.

The party camped nearby was made up of three hikers, Germans in their thirties, well-equipped with top notch backpacking gear— and those Sherpas they'd hired. That evening, we made a deal to join them. We would pay for the Sherpa's services. Our gear would go on the ponies. The Sherpas were willing, and the ponies could easily take what little we had. The Germans were nonplussed. Probably, they did not want these scruffy dirtbag hikers in their party. But we made it clear we did not want anything else from them, just to have the Sherpas help get our gear from camp to camp. That night we pitched our tent some ways away from the Germans, and the next morning, we all set out at the same time, much lighter for the help of the ponies.

The days were a strange mix of boredom and adventure. We walked all day, every day, mostly in silence, slightly ahead of the Germans. We did not talk with the Germans much because we wanted to avoid any sense that we were taking advantage of their well-appointed expedition. One day we split from the Sherpas, on their instruction. They would take the ponies one way while we short-cut across a series of hanging rope bridges. The ponies and our gear would be in camp when we arrived that afternoon.

At a river crossing, we watched while a Ladakhi man heaved bags of rice on his shoulders and navigated our first of a series of swinging bridges. Back and forth he went, hauling the fifty-pound bags from one side of the river to the other. When he was done, we went ourselves. The tangled strands of rope were rough under my hands and below, a white river rushed across the rocks. Because he was afraid of heights, Alastair hated these crossings. But there was no way to go but forward.

We navigated a thread of trail along a steep gravelly hillside, looking down to a ribbon of water that seemed miles below. Every now and then one of us would step too heavily, loosening an avalanche of stones far down into the valley. They were such long drops; the sound would stop long before the stones did. It was terrifying, and I could not help imagining myself falling. There was nothing to grab on to, I would slide for what must seem like hours before stopping, scraped and bleeding, on the banks of the river below. And then what? It would be impossible to get back up to the trail.

Some days we would cross those same rivers, stripping down and plunging into the ice-cold water, rich with glacial grit, our shoes and clothes on our heads. We'd be dry in no time on the other side, the air sucking every ounce of available moisture back into the environment.

We came across an empty temple, the square room silent and bare save for two red death's head masks hanging on a post in the middle of the room. I was a thief at heart for a mere moment, but I felt that if I even touched them, I would carry around some kind of curse for the rest of my life. Bad luck would follow me until I returned them to their home and how would I even find this place again? I circled the room and the masks watched me. Both the masks and the posts were painted the Tibetan red color that was so common. That red was everywhere, on the faces of angry gods, knitted into hats, carved into beads the shape of skulls and worn around the necks of Ladakhi women. It was the color of a monk's robes, and the color or the posts holding the roof up in a seemingly abandoned temple.

Our stove quit working entirely, and one evening, when there was no wood to be found for a fire, I wandered from our campsite to the nearby village to in hopes of finding a place to cook our dinner. There were no trees: of course, there was no wood for a fire. The local people would collect cow pies, let them dry, and burn them for fuel. I followed a footpath until I reached a cluster of houses, then knocked on the first door I found. I looked at the woman who opened it, realizing I had no words for what I wanted. I pointed at the pan I was carrying, a cheap aluminum thing with a wobbly lid and a flimsy wire handle. I peeked past her to the fire in their cavernous fireplace and pointed at the fire. She nodded at me and waved me in. The room was dark and warm and smoky, everything was heavy brown wood. She handed me a glass of tea and I smiled, and then I set my cooking pot in the fire. We sat there for half an hour in silence, just looking at each other. Me, this woman, two small children with those wind-chapped cheeks that showed the wear and tear of living in the mountains. When my dinner was done, I wrapped my scarf around the handle of the pan, nodded my thanks to the family, and headed back up into the meadow where we were camped.

I woke up the next day aching and weak. Everything hurt; I was barely able to move. The altitude had got the better of me. I struggled to make it through the day, at every step I wanted to curl up on the ground and go back to sleep. There was no turning back. We were days from anywhere, anything. I suffered through the day, every mile longer than the one before. That night, the Germans gave me some painkillers, but the next morning was just as bad. That was the day we had to cross the nearly 18,000-foot pass, the highest point in the journey. I could hardly lift my own weight to stand. I was too weak to even cry.

The Sherpas shifted some gear and loaded me on the back of one of the ponies. As we reached the pass, the snow became too deep; I had to walk the last mile or so to the top. Every step released the sound of breaking glass; it was the crunch of gravel and ice underfoot. My low sneakers were completely wrong and too slick on the bottom, but we reached the top—at 17,480 feet—with no incident. For a moment we stood in the wind, surrounded by a tumble of stones and faded prayer flags. The mountains spilled downhill around us in every direction. It should have been a celebratory moment. It should have been an accomplishment, but I was so exhausted that I could barely acknowledge where I was. I'd forgotten why I wanted so badly to be here, what it was I'd needed to prove.

I looked south, into the distance, tracing the line of the narrow brown trail with my eyes. It was all downhill from here. As soon as we got into lower altitudes and the air wasn't so thin, my strength returned enough to manage the long miles on foot again.

We parted with the Germans in Manali after paying the Sherpas and thanking them for delivering us safely. The sun had taken the skin off the bridge of my nose and the walking had taken any remaining meat from my bones. We went directly to a pizza place where the man working the counter said, "Oh, you have come over the mountains, haven't you?" We were ravenous and coated with dust and blasted by the sun and the wind. After scarfing down our dinner, we checked into a hotel and scrubbed the journey off before falling into a clean bed with a real mattress. It was a cheap guest house, but the room was large and clean and had a private bathroom. It seemed the peak of luxury. It was strange to look in a mirror. Alastair and I both wore the same wind-chapped faces the people in the mountains had. But my limbs were so thin. Every spare pound had been used as fuel for the journey.

Manali was a hill town like Shimla, a retreat for British colonists, and after independence, Indians escaped here to get away from the summer heat. It was also an ashram town—people came to practice yoga and sit with the guru of their choice. Travelers came from all over the world, and there were Indian pilgrims too. It was an easy place to land, a tourist town full of small hotels and restaurants that offered things familiar to Western travelers. It felt beyond luxurious to sleep inside, in a room with a bed and a private bathroom and running water.

We went to the movies in a small movie theater. They were showing *Chinatown* starring Jack Nicholas and Faye Dunaway. We were both hungry for pop culture after the silence and isolation of the mountains. We sat in the small dark theater until the movie reel caught fire and the managers told everyone they were sorry, that was all there was going to be, the movie was over. We walked out into the evening and back to our hotel, the mystery of how *Chinatown* ended completely unsolved. It didn't matter. Everything seemed so exciting: a movie, a restaurant, our room with running water. The walk had made the most mundane things precious.

But once the novelty of so much food and of sleeping in the same place every night began to wear off, Alastair's anger heated up again. I became confused about why I was still on the road. I was still sick, still losing weight. I felt like I might disappear if this kept up. I needed to stop being in motion just for the sake of movement.

But I could not settle in Manali. I was not going to join an ashram and sit in meditation while the days spooled out in front of me—how could that match the journey I had just taken? Crossing the Himalayas on foot was its own walking meditation. Our long days under those blue mountain skies had passed mostly in silence, Alastair's anger silenced by trail fatigue. Now that we were back in town, I spent hours doing nothing but reading the local newspapers. They were full of stories I did not understand, reports of people I had not heard of. I wasn't connected to this place like I'd been connected to Israel, there were no common threads.

What was I supposed to do with myself now? Was I going to get a job here in Manali? The hotels and hostels had no need of my services. They already spoke immaculate English and they knew how India worked. What contribution could I possibly make? And without an income, how would I sustain a life here?

Here in the Manali guest house, I felt all the miles of my travels catch up with me. So many hours standing on the side of the road, my bag at my feet, Alastair a few feet behind me, in the shadows so drivers wouldn't see him right away. So many nights sleeping rough and fending off Alastair's anger. I was fearless, open to strangers. Everyone but Alastair had been so kind.

"This is what it means when people say they love to travel," I thought. My head was full of the sound of languages I didn't know. I had seen the faces of hundreds of bodhisattvas on temple walls. I knew thrill of seeing a truck slow down to pick us up. I had let the magnetic pull of adventure take me and in return I had fallen in love with everything strange and beautiful and unknown, with the sheer joy of discovering anything new.

Without the energy to follow that call, my presence in this far away place served no purpose. I was a secondary character in a movie that would catch fire before we found out how it would end. The skinny American girl, the one from California with the mean English boyfriend. What was I doing on the edges like this? Why did I even appear in this story? I had done what I wanted to do. I had scraped the tips of my fingers on the blue Himalayan sky. What was next?

I flipped through my guidebook and calculated how much I would like to see the elaborately carved temples in Southern India. I considered what it would take to get there—the long train rides, the noisy stations, managing everything because the locals did not want to talk with Alastair. Alastair was still angry, and I was still lost. I needed education and guidance; I was not going to find it in the battered pages of my Lonely Planet guidebook.

The trip down to Delhi was a blur of buses winding down out of the mountains, and then, a night train. I looked out of my bunk to see a Sikh man standing in the aisle, his straight black hair hanging down past his waist. At the far end of the car, another man held the opposite end of the pale blue cloth he'd been wearing as a turban. They shook the fabric and folded it and pulled it tight. Then, the man with his hair down began to wrap the turban around his head.

In Delhi we checked into a hostel where the bunks were in rows on an open roof top, protected from the sun by fabric awnings. There was no privacy, but the patio was separated from the noise of the streets and it was an oasis in the chaos of New Delhi. We tried to explore the city, plunging into the Old Delhi market. I could not bear the onslaught of the noise, the crowds, the cows, the rickshaws, the constant motion around us. It was ten minutes, maybe fifteen, before I started to freak out. It was like being inside a machine, the noise was constant, the heat a blanket. After the quiet of the mountains, I didn't know how to be surrounded by all this activity.

"I have to go home," I told Alastair. He thought I meant back to the hostel. "Yes, I need to go back to the hostel," I said, "but I have to go home too." He blinked at me like he didn't understand what I had just said.

The next day, I found a travel agent and spent most of what was left of my money on a flight to London. We didn't talk about my almost immediate departure date. Early one morning, I took a taxi to the airport, leaving Alastair sleeping on the rooftop of the New Delhi hostel. I was not sad or angry or excited or broken hearted. I did not feel anything at all.

CHAPTER NINETEEN:
Back to the Gray

The Aeroflot plane was functional with its blue and gray décor. The flight attendants, in their boxy blue-gray uniforms, were functional. The stop in Tashkent was functional. There was nowhere to go, nothing to buy in the airport. Passengers waited in a concrete and glass box on the edge of the runway while more blue-gray crew members rolled out metal carts carrying glasses of apple juice. I sat on the blue-gray carpet, my legs stretched out in front of me, drank my juice, and waited while the plane refueled. Back on board, I leaned my head up against the window and watched the world turn dark below.

In Heathrow airport, I went to the tourist information desk and booked a shared room in a small hotel near Kensington Gardens. I took the Tube there as though I knew exactly where I was going. And I guess I did, from the months I spent wandering the city aimlessly while Alastair worked. It was early evening and two Australian girls were sitting on the other beds in the room chatting. I introduced myself and apologized, explaining that I'd just come from Delhi and I was beat. Would they forgive me if I just curled up and went to sleep? They were kind and quiet. I did not hear them when they skipped out for dinner, nor did I hear them when they came back a few hours later.

I woke up in the middle of the night, thirsty, hungry, and disoriented. I pulled on my clothes and wandered out to the lobby. Two young men were watching winter sports on the TV in the lobby, eating snacks and drinking tea. They were the night shift, both Nigerian. They told me this was what they did most nights: watched sports and greeted anyone who showed up after midnight. I told them I was hoping to find something to eat, and they invited me to sit with them for a while and share their snacks. One of them made me a cup of tea. We sat in the dim light of the lobby watching a downhill ski competition broadcast from somewhere—Switzerland, Austria, France, I don't know. I could not focus. After an hour or two, I thanked the guys and slipped back into my room. I was careful not to let too much light in and wake my roommates. I slept late into the morning and when I walked back into the lobby I wondered if I had been dreaming about watching skiing with the two Nigerian guys the night before. They were gone, replaced by a talkative Englishman with a cockney accent.

I did not have enough money to get back to California, and I was not quite ready to call home, so I called Alastair's parents instead. I had left some of my things at their house. I wanted to go get them, and I wanted to find Alastair's friend, Stuart, who I'd met when we lived in Brixton and liked. I was hoping to stay with him until I figured out how to get home.

"Oh, it's you," said Alastair's mom when she opened the door. I'd taken the train up, and she invited me in and fed me dinner. We walked over to Stuart's parents' house, just a few doors down, so I could get Stuart's phone number. That evening, I called Stuart and asked if I could crash at his place while I figured out how to get home.

Stuart said I could have the couch for a few days and gave me his address.

For the duration of my short stay with them, Alastair's parents looked at me like they were not sure who I was or why I was there. I felt like a stray kitten they'd found in their backyard. They would feed me and let me sleep in a box in the garage, but first thing in the morning, I was going to the pound. Alastair's dad took me to the post office to ship my belongings home, the things I could not fit in my bag, and then to the train station to buy a ticket back to London.

I was glad to leave Alastair's parents. They reminded me of him, and the quiet in their home was unsettling. For a moment I felt something like sympathy for Alastair, who had his mother's eyes and hair and his father's severe mouth. I wondered if his father was as mean to his mother as Alastair was to me, if that's where he learned it was acceptable to hit another human in anger. Their lives seemed comfortable, but also so silent. Maybe their lives shattered with the same kind of anger Alastair had, whenever his father got angry.

I wanted to tell Alastair's mother that her son had hit me, often, and I wanted to ask her if she knew where he had learned that. I wanted to ask her if she suffered the same treatment, but I lost my nerve. Where would this painful revelation get either of us? Maybe she would apologize to me for Alastair's behavior, but if she was a victim of the same, would the understanding be enough? I wanted Alastair's parents to make something right for me, even if I wasn't sure what it was. But as soon as his mother said, "Oh, it's you," at the door, I knew this was a ridiculous idea. I wanted to get my things—my useless things. I had so little, I don't know why I bothered. I wanted to get away from these people who had made Alastair what he was.

Alastair's father had gone to work early in the morning, so I shook hands with his mother on the front porch and walked out of the subdivision to the bus that would take me to the train to London. Later that day I climbed the stairs to Stuart's apartment, a place he shared with two roommates. They knew Alastair and were welcoming.

I assumed I would know what to do once I'd got to London, but I was wrong. I'd forgotten I couldn't get a job. I didn't have a work permit. If I found work, where was I going to live? After the weekend was over, Stuart told me his roommates were asking how long I planned to stay. I was not paying rent, just taking up space. I was trying to stay out of the way, but I was just a freeloader. I found a bank where I asked about receiving money from overseas. It would take a week, maybe two; my dad would have to fill out some paperwork. I had no other choices. I called my dad.

"Things are very complicated here," he said. "So, I just want to warn you before you come home. We moved and . . . it's complicated. You might want to reconsider."

I talked to my stepmom too. "Are you sure you want to come here?" she said. "It's . . . yeah."

I did not know what my either of them meant, and they did not offer clarification. "No. I need to come home. I can't stay here." I insisted. "I can't work, and I don't have a place to live." I would not have said it out loud, but I desperately needed someone to take care of me and my dad felt like the only person I could expect this from.

"Okay," he said, "but things are... different. You might want to figure something else out."

Stuart was inviting me to tag along on nights out, but ten days had gone by and I had worn out my welcome. I knew that. He was nice to me because he still saw me as Alastair's girlfriend. But he could not have me there rent-free. It was not fair. I wondered what he would say if I told him the truth about Alastair. Would he apologize for rushing me and tell me to take all the time I needed? But it wasn't his mess to clean up, it wasn't his fault. All these times I wanted to tell someone, anyone, about what I'd been through.

It wasn't just Alastair's violent temper, though that was a big part of it. I wanted to talk about the sound of air raid sirens in Israel. How Eli broke my heart. Older things, too, about how I'd been moved three times during that year of high school, how Casey's parents thought I was the problem. I wanted someone to listen to me. Someone to believe that my skinny legs had carried me over the highest of mountain passes, or that I had hitchhiked the length of a Greek island alone looking for work. It never felt right, my own stories didn't feel true even to me. And I couldn't bear the idea that anyone would feel sorry for me.

I hated that Stuart was leaning on me about my plans, even while I knew he was right, that I was being a bad guest. I told him I would be out as soon as the money came from my dad. I needed to find another place to stay as soon as possible. I needed to go home. I didn't matter what was happening back in California. I couldn't be a tourist forever, and certainly not on the good graces of others.

A few days before the money came in, we went out with another one of Alastair's friends and got kind of drunk. Miles was fair skinned and witty, and he couldn't or wouldn't go home. Stuart gave Miles a blanket that had not quite dried from the laundry and put him on the floor next to the couch where I'd been sleeping. We were talking and then he asked me to share my blanket with him. Alastair had told me about Miles, how he was always hitting on any available girl, and doing a very bad job of it. So now, here he was, hitting on me. I did not think twice about it, and then we were undressed and Miles was trying to fuck me, and failing. I was barely present for the process. I was not interested in sex, but I did not mind either. It would be easy to say I was going along out of revenge, because I wanted to hurt Alastair, but I did not feel that strongly about anything.

Then Miles apologized.

"I seem to be having an attack of guilt," he said. "I should not be trying to fuck my friend's girlfriend."

"Oh, don't feel guilty," I replied, "He was awful to me. I'm not his girlfriend anymore."

"I'm sorry," he said, sounding like he meant it.

Maybe we would have been friends had things been different, had we not been drunk, had I not been so displaced. I did not tell him about Alastair's temper, about how he hit me when he was angry, about how no one would talk to him in India. I didn't tell him how I imagined the Indian people we met could somehow see his character in ways that I had not been able to. I did not share the specifics, but it was the first time I'd ever approached saying the truth out loud.

Miles rented an apartment, he lived alone, and he had a good job. I wanted him to invite me to stay with him, but I did not ask. It was too weird, especially after he'd been trying to fuck me. I stayed with Stuart and his roommates for a few more days, trying to be out of the house as much as possible, taking the bus every day to the bank to see if the money my dad wired had come in.

When it finally arrived, I bought a nice bottle of booze for Stuart and his roommates. It wasn't enough—I knew that. Everyone had gone to work when I left, and I was relieved to slip out so easily. I didn't want to admit how much I'd taken advantage of these generous people. I didn't want them to know how much they had saved me from being broke on the streets of London. I left a thank you note and went back to the little hotel where I'd spent my first nights in London. I stayed there until my flight left for California. I did not see the nightshift guys. I had adjusted to London time, and if they were watching late night sports, I did not know because I was sleeping.

CHAPTER TWENTY:
Not Quite Home

God, I hated Orange County. I hated everything about it. I hated the beige suburbs, I hated the eight-lane arterials. I hated the color of the sky. I had a job I hated, at a chain pizza restaurant just a few miles from the house, and I went to the community college that was far away, so I hated the commute. I carpooled with my neighbor in his raised four-wheel-drive pickup truck. I hated that pickup truck. Why was it so far off the ground? I hated driving everywhere. I hated the traffic. I especially hated the supermarket. I hated shopping, and once, I burst into tears in the shampoo aisle. How could there be so many kinds of shampoo? Who needed so many choices? Why were there so many cars? Where the hell was everyone going all the time?

It took three rounds of medication clear up my guts for good. I was still fighting giardia and salmonella, and I had wasted away to a mere ninety-six pounds. I was exhausted all the time, and I was culture shocked as all get out.

It seemed like no one cared where I'd been the last year and a half. No one asked me about the war in Israel or the sky over the Himalayas or the color of the child-bride's eyes in Pakistan. Nothing I'd seen felt real. I went to Philosophy 101 and English Composition at the college and I quit my job at the pizza place when my manager gave my phone number out to one of his friends. I got a job at a florist in a strip mall where I liked my boss and my coworkers and the guy that drove the delivery van. I knew where I was supposed to be every day and when I was supposed to be there.

Inside I was still lost all the time. I'd dropped from months of wandering at whatever pace the day demanded into this regimented but pointless existence. It should have been easy for me to settle. I understood the language, I knew how things worked, and there was an order to my daily life. But I could see no point in anything—not school, not work, nothing. I felt disconnected from normal life activities. I was acting out the life of a community college student living with her dad and her stepmom, working a decent part-time job. It was good, I guess, normal, but it felt like someone else was living all of this for me. I liked my classes, I liked the reading and the writing and the academic parts of school, but the broad concrete plazas at the community college overwhelmed me and I was impatient with my classmates. My California upbringing had been interrupted with experiences that I didn't share with anyone.

At home, the television was on all the time. My stepmom was watching the stock markets, the financials. I didn't know what any of that was. Dad was coming and going, I'm not sure to or from where. I hung out with my little brother and the dogs. When I didn't have work or school, sometimes I'd go to the beach and spend the night with Kevin, a guy I was hooking up with when he wasn't with his girlfriend. I went out with him because he didn't want anything, and he was shockingly good looking. He was at loose ends too. He waited tables and got good tips, partly because of his looks. He could have been a model, but he had no ambition. All he wanted to do with his time was play tennis, swim in the ocean, and get laid.

I thought it wasn't the worst possible set of priorities, given that I had no idea what I was doing, either. I would drive over to Kevin's house and we would talk and get high and shoehorn ourselves his single bed. He lived with his mom. He'd kind of washed up on her porch after his own getting busted for selling weed at his last job. He wasn't particularly criminal, he was just a surfer boy who wanted easy money.

I met Kevin's girlfriend a few times. She was skinny, had perfect makeup and was always talking about something she'd seen on TV. She reminded me a little bit of Lauren, my first kibbutz roommate. I didn't like her much, but she deserved better than to be with a guy who was cheating on her with me. Kevin and his girlfriend were in my neighborhood one night when I'd been stood up for a date. They dropped by the house to see what I was up to. Kevin started talking about how he was jealous I had a date; he wouldn't stand me up if it were him. I stopped hanging out with him after that. I knew I shouldn't have been with him in the first place. He hadn't made his girlfriend a secret to me, but he didn't tell her that we were sleeping together. I wasn't jealous but after he started acting possessive of me in front of his girlfriend, I felt bad. He was never going to be honest with her. Seeing that made me feel like a jerk and I called the whole thing off.

On my days off, I would ride my bike through the suburbs of Orange County, spinning my wheels over mile after mile of asphalt shoulder, past subdivision after subdivision after subdivision. I went to the movies alone, often. I took my little brother to the playground. I took the dogs for long walks. I wrote my philosophy papers and English essays, and I got good grades. Sometimes, I'd go to parties with the delivery van driver from the flower shop and he'd flirt with me. I didn't take him seriously because he flirted with everybody. He was always handing out flowers to women he thought were pretty while he was on delivery runs.

I liked hanging out with him because his world was different than all the beige of Orange County. He shared a house with a Chilean astrophysics student and another guy from Germany. Ernst was an aircraft engineer who was working on an ultra-light airplane in a warehouse behind a black Baptist church. These guys were from a larger world than most of the people I met in my daily life. Talking with them made me feel like the places I'd been were real. They were impressed that I had so many miles on me, and I liked that.

I went to bed with the Chilean guy one night after we all had dinner together. It was mean because Ernst had an obvious crush on me. But Ernst reminded me so much of Alastair that I could hardly stand to think of him that way. One day Ernst showed me his passport and I gasped with recognition. I dug out a photo I had of Alastair and held it up against Ernst's passport photo. He could have been Alastair's brother. They had the same sunken eyes, the same long limbs, and it didn't help that Ernst had that same immaculate British-accented English.

I wanted to be friends with Ernst, and I genuinely enjoyed his company. Once he accepted that we weren't ever going to be a thing, I brought him home to have dinner with my dad and stepmom. They were enchanted; Ernst was smart and interesting, and he was Jewish, too, on top of everything else—exactly the boyfriend they'd have chosen for me, minus the motorcycle he rode.

I floated through my days with no particular goals, no particular direction. It would be wrong to say I was bored, though certainly I found nearly everything boring. It was more complicated than that. I guess my stepmom noticed my listlessness and she scheduled an appointment for me with her therapist. He was a pleasant man with a reddish blonde beard. I liked talking to him because he asked me what I had been doing for the past few years. It seems ridiculous that someone had to pay a guy to ask me this, but no one else was doing it. It was a relief to have someone—anyone—ask. But one night, I was in my bedroom and I overheard my stepmom say that she and my dad could not go out as planned. "She can't be left alone," my stepmom said. "The therapist says she's suicidal."

I was hot with rage. She was wrong. I couldn't believe that the therapist—the guy who was supposed to be a trained professional—was so wrong too. Shouldn't he know better? And why hadn't anyone just, you know, asked me if I'd been thinking of killing myself? The idea got more and more ridiculous the longer I rolled it around in my head. I was depressed, certainly. I did not want this specific life, directionless in the suburbs of Orange County. That was one hundred percent true. But I had not figured out what my life was yet. There was no way I was interested in ending it. It was such a frustrating piece of information to have, this news of my suicidal nature. I had a place to sleep, I had food and medical care, I was in college, and I was working. Things should have improved. But once I learned I was supposedly unstable and should be treated as such, it felt like I had to start over. Again.

The van driver from the flower shop got fired. He'd been using the van as his own transportation when he wasn't on the clock. After he lost his job, he just disappeared. He'd packed up his stuff and he was gone. His room in the house he shared with Ernst and the Chilean guy was empty. On a hot afternoon while my stepmom was out shopping with my little brother and my dad was doing whatever it was he did, I threw my belongings in the car. I dumped my bags on the sagging single bed left in the van driver's empty bedroom. Then I took the car back and rode my bike across the flat, wide streets to the

Latino neighborhood where the house was. The guys needed a room-mate and I needed a place to live where people were not mistaking my culture shock and depression for suicidal tendencies.

It wasn't a great idea. The neighborhood was rough, and the house had been broken into twice. The second time all of the stereo equipment was stolen. But I'd been in worse places. There were some weird household dynamics—the Chilean guy had a gorgeous girlfriend who'd showed up from somewhere and Ernst was frustrated with me a lot of the time because he did not want to be just friends. It would have to do.

Everything that had become normal to me—the endless challenges of travel, Alastair's fist meeting the soft part of my upper arm, not knowing where I'd be sleeping one night to the next, even the bombs falling from over the Israel-Lebanon border—were not things that should have been normal to anyone. And the things that were normal—the traffic of Orange County, the nonstop consumerism, day jobs and supermarkets and television—felt wrong and ill-fitting. At least sharing this house with these two foreign guys, I would have room to be myself in ways that weren't being analyzed.

I called my dad. "I ran away from home," I said. "I'm not suicidal. I just don't understand how anything works. Nothing feels like mine."

"Okay," he said. "You should bring Ernst to dinner again. He's a great guy."

Once again, it seemed like I could have said anything, anything at all. It would have netted the same reaction. I ran off to join the circus. I'm going to work in porn. I'm pregnant with twins; I'm not sure who the father is. No one paid one bit of attention to what I was really saying.

Maybe it *was* my fault. Maybe I should have known enough to say, "I'm pretty depressed. I've been through some shit, and I don't know what to make of any of it." But it's not clear even that would have helped. And I didn't know how to say it.

"I'll come pick up the rest of my things this weekend," I said, and I hung up the phone.

In many ways, this no man's land of Orange County turned out to be the worst place I'd been yet. It is a strange thing to say after I had left a warzone, an abusive boyfriend, and a tenacious illness behind, but homogeneity can really bring you down. In other places, there were good reasons for feeling displaced or different or scared or confused about the basics of how things worked. I wasn't from there. I didn't speak the language. I didn't expect to know what was going to happen one day to the next. Even during the fairly scheduled days on kibbutz—days uninterrupted by rockets—you could find you'd been reallocated. You'd work the laundry one day, the fields the next, or you were expected stuff live chickens into crates while squinting into the headlights of a front-loader in the middle of the night. But here, this was supposed to be my home. I should have been able to figure it out.

Orange County had the Santa Ana winds; they reminded me of the desert winds in Israel. The air would get hot and everything would turn the same color as the houses, the sand color of stuccoed housing development walls and concrete sidewalks was everywhere. I'd feel the grit in my eyelashes and between my teeth. It was hard to get anything done when the Santa Anas were blowing. It was oppressive—this feeling like there was no difference between the sky and the ground. It was draining to look up at the sun, the sickly light leaking through the pale filter of the desert sands, to bake in the relentless heat. It was no good for biking because the air tasted bad. The heat held after dark, too, and I could not shake the feeling of being cooked from the inside out. When the Santa Ana winds blew, it erased the differences between everything. The whole county was washed in sameness.

My roommates were an island of brightness in a place where most of my life seemed relentlessly dull. On my Sundays off from the flower shop, I would get on the back of Ernst's motorcycle and he would take me to his workshop behind the Baptist church. The music would fly out of the church and into the tilted open windows of the shop. I would sit and read while Ernst patiently added layers of fiberglass to the experimental glider he was building. Sometimes, the three of us went to parties with other South Americans, great, meaty BBQs with cheerful, stocky men and beautiful women, and I would try to use my rusty Spanish.

One night Ernst got mad at me because the guy working the late-night donut shop didn't speak English, and I said, out loud, "I don't think he speaks very much English." Ernst was outraged and went on a tirade about Americans and our provincial attitude. I was flustered by this. I didn't care that the guy didn't speak English; it was just an explanation for why the transaction was slow. I was disappointed to see in Ernst that same judgmental streak that I'd seen in so many of the Germans I met while traveling, I was disappointed that he needed to lecture me. He was the closest thing to a friend I had in Orange County. But in this moment, he was another guy judging me for failing his expectations, expectations I didn't even know about.

My failings didn't stop Ernst from asking me to marry him. His visa was going to expire at some point, and he wanted to stay in the United States. Ernst had no income. I was working at the florist and paying for community college myself. In our barely furnished shared house in this working-class immigrant suburb, it never occurred to me that Ernst could be from a wealthy family.

That changed when he told me that his father would pay for everything. He told me his family would like me, a well-traveled Jewish girl, so I should not worry about my financial-aid status. It was all a simple transaction: I would marry Ernst, he would get US residency, and I would get my education paid for. I'd remembered what I'd learned when Alastair and I considered this choice. It wasn't so simple. I would not be able to prove myself capable of supporting Ernst when it came down to it, but he told me it wouldn't matter, his father had the money to guarantee our support. I liked the idea of not worrying about paying for college, of having some financial support, but it was too complicated. I said no.

I worked. I rode my bike. I went out to the bars with one of my coworkers from the flower shop and her girlfriends. I got paid every two weeks and I paid my rent. I occasionally went to have dinner with my family. I was living, I was safe, but I didn't know what I wanted. Nothing seemed like it was leading to anything else. There was no pass to cross, no train station to navigate, no reason to do anything at all.

I was in a constant state of grief for the magical maze of unpredictability that had been my daily life while I was traveling. I was broken hearted about Alastair because the loss of something bad in your life is still a loss. He was the person I'd gone overland through Pakistan with, the only other keeper of those memories. I was constantly aware of the empty space he used to fill. I felt blurry, an out-of-focus photograph. I still lived like a backpacker, but I wasn't going anywhere.

Shortly before I moved out of my dad and my stepmom's place, I had an accident and totaled their late-seventies Volvo sedan. My dad had been driving a late-model Dodge Dart, a car that was my grandfather's. He'd brought it out from New York after my grandfather died. The car still had my grandfather's name on it and sometimes we would get phone calls from people asking for my grandfather by name.

"He's not here," I'd say, "he died a few years ago. What's this about?" There'd be an exasperated sigh on the other end of the line, and then, they'd hang up.

I knew something was up, but that's all I knew. One afternoon, I had been flipping through the newspaper to find another used car; the plan was to spend the insurance money from the totaled sedan. I asked my dad about making some calls. I'd done the research and narrowed it down to a few possible options. When I asked about answering the ads I'd circled in the paper, my dad yelled at me. "That money is going to lawyers, not to another car."

He didn't elaborate. I didn't ask. I was stunned by his reaction. I folded the newspaper and went to my room. Not so long after that, my dad was indicted by the federal government for selling electronic equipment to a dealer in Hong Kong. That same gear ended up in Pakistan where it was illegal under some Reagan-era cold-war nuclear laws. The law had been circling around them for a while now, making their lives uncertain. My dad yelling at me about the insurance pay-out from the accident was the first time I realized something very bad was happening with them. It was the first time I realized they had been ignoring my struggles because their own issues were so all consuming.

Before I moved in with Ernst and the Chilean guy, I'd been fighting with my stepmom about the trivialities of shared space. I'd leave a glass on the side table next to my bed, a washcloth on the edge of the sink. These careless behaviors upset her. When she would scold me, I would think about air-raid sirens, about how we scrambled down the stairs in that apartment building in Nahariya, leaving dinner on the table, half-eaten plates of food just sitting there. I would squint at my stepmom's frustration, trying to see what she was so upset about. And I'd hear a voice in my head telling me I did not belong here. That voice wasn't angry or sad or imbalanced, there was nothing creepy or crazy about it. It was like a radio announcer reading the weather. It's going to rain, take an umbrella. Thing is, the voice was right, I did not belong. My stepmom had made the effort to include me in her life with my dad, she helped me recover my health, and her taking me to the therapist was part of that. But despite her efforts, it was clear that I was a problem that she would rather have go away.

It was good not to be sixteen anymore, so when I squinted sideways at my stepmom's reaction to my presence, I realized that I could just go somewhere else. It was a smaller journey than winging away from New Delhi, leaving Alastair and his anger behind, but it was the same desire to survive that sent me back out into the world again.

As my first term in college was coming to an end, I looked at my life that same way, trying to make sense of what I was doing. Ernst was my only real friend, the only person who I could just hang out with. But he kept asking me about marriage. I knew how he felt about me, what he thought I could do for him. I wasn't sure I wanted to be part of that. I liked working in the flower shop and I loved my boss, a towering woman with frosted hair and a raunchy sense of humor. But it was just a job, the kind of job I could find anywhere. I could continue my classes at any community college. I didn't have to stay in this beige landscape where so much of my life was dependent on having a car and the only place the strip malls ended was where Orange County fell into the ocean. I called my mom. She was living in the Bay Area, where I'd gone to high school, where I'd hung out with Mackey and Ian.

I finished the semester at community college, quit my job at the flower shop, told my roommates I was leaving. I moved back to Northern California—back to the place where my trip started.

CHAPTER TWENTY-ONE:
Back Where I Started

It hurt what little pride I had to ask my mom if I could stay with her while I figured out what to do next. I didn't know where else to go. Ian had disappeared into San Francisco and Mackey was still living with her parents, though she was spending most of her time with her boyfriend. I needed to land somewhere. I asked, even though it was hard, and I planned to get back on my feet as quickly as possible.

It turned out okay. My stepfather helped me get a job at a deli owned by a friend. Later, he brought me up to the university to look at the housing board, so I could find a place to live. I registered for the local community college and started classes. I went to back riding my bike everywhere and hanging out with old friends.

Mackey worked in salon doing manicures and her nails were always perfect. I never understood why this was what she'd decided to do with herself. But didn't matter because she didn't understand what I'd been up to either. Her unquestioning company didn't feel like a lack of interest, it felt like she just accepted who I was and what I'd done. The least I could do was give her the same in return. We went back to driving around in her car, going to record stores to spend her money on new music that I picked out, and sitting in bars looking at cute guys, because now we were old enough to do that.

I took the smallest room in a house I shared with two Stanford students, one studying physics, the other studying classics. My roommates were interesting and interested and we had an easy life sharing our three-bedroom, one-bathroom home. Everyone paid their rent on time, and we all got on so well that we started having weekly dinners. We'd rotate whose night it was to cook. We'd invite friends over, play records—the house was always full of Emmy Lou Harris's voice—and drink beer in the back yard. Our biggest conflict was over the bathroom—there was only the one—and even that wasn't a big deal because we all had different schedules. We had a cat named Harris who liked to hang on the screen door and leave us dead birds on the mat.

There were always Stanford students around. I envied them their top-notch educations and their teaching assistant positions and how they didn't seem to have jobs like I did, jobs where they were on their feet all day. They didn't come home from work smelling like lunch meat. But they were open and fun to be around. I never felt like a second-class citizen because I worked in a deli or my education was at the community college. One of my roommates set me up with an astrophysicist and we dated for a while. He was so good looking— he'd turned down a swimming scholarship to study physics at Stanford and to my surprise, he seemed to really like me. It fizzled out because he met someone while doing research in Germany, but he was never mean, even when he told me he'd met someone else.

I started knocking off the essentials at community college so I could transfer to university. My high school grades weren't good enough to get me admitted without doing some catch-up work. All those years skipping class had caught up with me, but I enjoyed the community college. I enjoyed getting up at six and riding my bike up to campus to attend the seven o'clock English composition class.

Money was very tight, but I didn't feel poor. I ate well, I had a comfortable place to live, I paid my rent, and I lived within my means. But paying for college was hard. It stretched what little I earned to the absolute maximum. I applied for financial aid. Even though it was only a few hundred dollars, a tuition waiver would make a huge difference.

My application was rejected. I didn't understand. I was working a minimum-wage job, and I met all the guidelines. Though I never felt deprived, I was earning just enough money to survive. I went to the financial aid office to appeal and the aid officer, a large, soft-voiced man, told me that I had been rejected because my father had claimed me as a dependent on his tax returns. I burst into tears. I was so embarrassed that I was crying in this man's office—and furious with my father. It seemed outrageous that he could claim he was support-ing me. It had been true in the recent past, in the six months I'd lived Southern California. He'd provided a roof over my head and my medical care when I got back from India. He'd paid for my flight home from London.

But I'd paid my college tuition out of money I earned at the pizza place and then the florist. I'd paid my rent and my share of the bills when I lived in that dumpy shared house in Santa Ana. I was paying my own way still. I explained all of this to the aid officer while trying to control my tears. The financial aid officer believed me. Okay, maybe he just wanted me to stop crying, but he overruled the rejec-tion and approved my application for aid. He slid a box of Kleenex across his desk towards me and told me he would fix everything.

I finally felt like my life was mine. I was in school, I had a decent job, I liked my roommates. I'd had a nice boyfriend who showed me that having a nice boyfriend was possible, something I didn't think would ever happen for me. I didn't mind being single. It was fine to be alone. Things made a weird kind of sense. I had a plan of sorts, and basic things, like where I was going to sleep, where the money would come from, weren't worrying me. I wasn't lost in the world anymore.

When Alastair appeared on my back patio, I didn't know what to say. I couldn't quite believe he was standing there. I had been sitting out back after work, reading, and I hadn't heard the doorbell ring. I blinked at him like he was a mirage, but he did not go away. I was home alone. Both of my roommates were gone. I was afraid. But mostly, I was angry.

"This is where you live," Alastair said to me, stating the obvious. I kept looking at him, tilting my head, and wondering how he could be in my yard. He had that same long-limbed swing in his body, the looseness in his joints that caught my eye when I watched him dance. But I did not find it appealing at all. I could only think of what happened when he'd swing an arm my way, his fist making contact with my skin. He was dressed almost exactly as I had seen him last, in running shorts and a pale blue t-shirt that was ragged around the collar. He had not shaved. He was deeply tanned but still had the same dark circles around his sunken blue eyes.

"How did you find me?"

"I went to your mom's house. That's the address I had for you. They told me where you were."

"What are you doing here?"

"Eileen told me you'd written that you missed me," he said.

I didn't answer. Eileen—Alastair's friend who got me through my time in the hospital in Jerusalem—and I still traded postcards now and then. But it had been months since I'd heard from anyone from my traveling days.

I was in no hurry to say anything. I missed the excitement of the road and the high Himalayan sky. I missed the feeling of romance that Paris held, and I missed taking the subway to London's sprawling museums. I missed eating avocado omelets during the harvest in Israel and I missed the feeling of the dry hot sun hitting the orchards after waking up in the dark. I missed watching the landscape roll by outside the window of a long-distance bus or train, the cheerful good-natured truck drivers who picked us up at the side of the road and blasted bouzouki music so loud it hurt my ears. I missed Ronnie's raunchy sense of humor. I missed Eli's open-hearted way of talking with strangers and I missed his mom's Friday afternoon baklava. But I didn't miss Alastair. It turns out you can miss the life you had with someone, things about that life, and not miss the person at all.

I stood up and made sure I was out of arm's reach. I looked at Alastair some more. What on earth was he doing here?

"Can I see your house?" he asked.

I tried to process that he was standing in my back yard. I shook my head. Not like you shake your head "no," but like you shake your head when you're trying to figure something out.

"Could I get a glass of water?" He was waiting for me to say something. Anything.

"Come inside." He followed me through the sliding glass door to the kitchen, where he eyed the bottles of liquor above the kitchen cabinets. I handed him a glass of water.

"Are those real?" he asked, waving a hand at the liquor bottles. I felt like I was looking at him through fog. "She said you wanted to see me," he tried again. "I really missed you."

Something inside me shifted. I repeated his words inside my head. "She said you wanted to see me." I could imagine writing that I missed Alastair, but it felt like I was remembering something I'd read somewhere, not an experience I'd personally experienced.

I felt ambushed. In my kitchen, the kitchen I shared with my roommates, people who were my friends, he looked like an intruder. He hadn't written to ask me if he could come, he just showed up. Fuck this, I thought. No.

"You can't be here," I said.

This wasn't what he'd been expecting. I was surprised by my own solidity, my own insistence. "You have to leave. You can't stay here." I walked over to the front door and opened it. He took his long strides behind me. I was afraid he would take a swing at me, but he didn't. He put his arms out and asked for a hug. I gritted my teeth and let him hold me for a few seconds and then, I stepped back and said, for the last time, "You have to leave. Now. I don't want you here."

He walked out the front door and I closed it behind him, locking it. Then I went in the back yard and smoked cigarettes, one after the other, until it got dark.

CHAPTER TWENTY-TWO:
The Same River Twice

It's not like I told Alastair to leave and was all of a sudden a person who had her shit together—full of power and in control of my life. It took years of bad decisions and regret until I felt like I'd solidified in some way. It took years until I even knew what questions to ask about how I'd ended up so far beyond the margins of the world I had grown up in.

Did my parents think it was okay for me to be in a warzone? Were they willfully ignoring the news, or did they just not know what was happening? Were their own worries so intense that it was okay to just stop raising me, and let the world do it for them? Was I, at seventeen, eighteen, wise enough to make smart decisions about what my path would be? Or was I so difficult that it was easier to let me fall off the map?

Even after I learned the truth about my dad's problems with the law, I bounced back and forth between feeling like my parents had either overestimated my ability to cope in the world and feeling like they didn't care.

I received a letter from Alastair maybe a month after he'd been to see me. It was mailed to my mom's house. She handed it to me and without even opening it, I tore it up and threw it away, right then and there, mashing the tiny pieces in with the food garbage so I wouldn't be tempted to pick it out later and piece it together.

"Do you want to tell me about it?" my mom asked.

"It was bad," I said. "And no, I don't want to talk about it."

My dad went to prison. I suppose I really was more than he could take on. Everything was more than he could take on. My step-mom served time, too, in a halfway house. I did not visit my dad in jail, not once, though I wrote to him. He served most of his time in a minimum-security facility with a bunch of corrupt Wall Street traders. But once he spent a few weeks in an overcrowded lock-up in Los Angeles where they'd sent him to have surgery for a hernia. He came out of prison having found religion in a bigger way than he'd had before, wearing a yarmulke and a ponytail, and as a member of Toastmasters, a public-speaking club that did workshops in his prison.

During my first semester in college, I had to write a paper for my philosophy class. I was full of half-baked versions of complex ideas, a weird mix of Tibetan Buddhist, fatalism, and European socialism. I got an A, but I also got a note from the instructor saying that it helped him understand who I was, how I was in his class. I was full of questions, well-read, well-traveled, but with no skills to analyze what I'd seen. That philosophy class was the first place I'd been where it was okay to try to make sense of the world and not have it be a big deal. It was okay to ask questions and to say that things seemed fucked up—that was the whole point.

For many years, I carried around the weight of the mistakes I'd made. I wanted to go back in time and undo them. I wanted to go back to that first summer when the bombs started to fall, tell my parents that they were crazy. I was seventeen, in a warzone, why weren't they insisting I come home? I wanted to push Hannes off me, and then, the next day, when he blamed me for his bad behavior, I wanted to say, "Fuck you, you're the one who was drunk and crawled into my bed. What the fuck was that? Fuck you." The first time Alastair's temper appeared, I wanted to pick up my things, go back to my room, and never speak to him again.

I wanted to erase all the bad things that had happened. I wanted to rewrite so much of my past. I wanted a normal gap year, where I slept in hostels and met other travelers and kissed strangers in far-away places. Where I came back home a tiny bit worldlier with ideas about European socialism and public transportation, but unscarred. I wanted to do the impossible, to go back and change my response at every critical junction in my timeline, to say how I really felt—scared, directionless, badly in need of guidance—instead of believing that no one cared so it was better for me to say I was fine.

Saying I was fine prevented everyone else from telling me what I thought would be the answer if I admitted I need help. I was afraid that answer would be *no*, that I wasn't good enough to help, that I deserved everything I'd received. For many years, I was filled with regret for not saving myself, and for not believing that anyone else would if I asked them to.

Because I work as a writer and a lot of my work is online, I'm not hard to find. People look me up and appear in my inbox at random.

A childhood friend. Someone I met while traveling, years back. Old roommates I've lost touch with. It's not surprising that Alastair found me, though I would never have expected him to contact me; over twenty years had passed. I saw the "from" line on my screen and debated for a while if I should open the email at all, or just go outside. I took a deep breath and opened the email.

He'd found my blog and apparently spent a great deal of time reading it. "People don't change, do they?" he'd said.

I looked at my screen, at his name at the bottom of the note. "Oh, but you're wrong," I said out loud, to myself. "They do. They really, really do. They become themselves. No matter how hard you try, you cannot stop them." Then I deleted the email and went for a walk.

I recently sliced open the tape on a box I had not opened since two or three addresses back. I went to the basement and found my past in all its Kodachrome four-by-six print glory. I found a picture of myself as an exchange student in Sweden. I am surrounded by pale blondes and I look so different from everyone around me, compact with an impressive shag of black hair. There is a picture of me standing in the Negev in Israel. There are no distinguishing landmarks, but I know exactly when it was by how strong I look. I was a poster child for a bright Israeli future, no matter that I had no intention of staying in Israel, no matter that the country had told me my time was up. There are pictures of Alastair, his deep-set steely blue eyes. When I look at the photos I imagine I can see that looseness in his joints too. I found just a few pictures of myself in India, stick-skinny and serious.

I wonder what it would be like to do that trip again, though it is impossible. The trek that I took on foot in India, that trip can be made by road now in a day. Many of the *kibbutzim* have been broken up, privatized. That way of life doesn't exist as it did when I was in Israel. I suspect vacation homes occupy the entire beach front of that town on Corfu. The suburbs of Cairo must sprawl almost to the feet of the Sphinx, the splendid frescoed tombs in the Valley of the Kings are likely untouchable behind protective barriers. I would never be lost; the mysteries of my location would be solved by my phone.

There's a quote attributed to Heraclitus, the Greek philosopher: No one ever steps in the same river twice, for it's not the same river and she's not the same person. Retracing my steps might help me remember what had happened more accurately, or maybe not, because time is sure to have rendered everywhere I was before completely unrecognizable. Time has rendered me unrecognizable too, I imagine. During recent travels, I was in a train station in Barcelona, and I saw a man who was the spitting image of Alastair—the Alastair from my memory. I felt a moment of fear in that recognition, and then I realized, no, that's not possible. I am so much older now, and he would be too; Alastair could not have escaped time any more than I have.

I wish I had not been so afraid to speak about what was happening to me while it was happening, I wish I had been able to extend the trust I felt towards strangers on the road, who were almost always so generous and kind. I wish I had told them I needed more than a ride; I needed a rescue. But there is no rewriting the past; there is only the fading of time and memory.

Right next to that feeling of regret, is one of sheer wonder for what my travels gave me. Really good baklava transports me to Eli's kitchen, his mom cutting the corner piece out just for me. The sound of the sitar finds me in my bunk in the mountain guest house, looking out the window watching the mist coat the trees. A warm shift in the wind and I feel the delight of sitting high above the road with a cheerful truck driver, the music much too loud, the landscape rolling past. There is a certain blueness in the summer sky in Seattle, a saturation.

In that color, in the outline of the Olympic Mountains on the horizon, I see the Himalayas. I picture a dusty line of trail scratched into the earth. A silver ribbon of river runs far below me, and as it changes, so do I.

Apologies and
Acknowledgements

I figure the people in this book don't exist anymore. We're all so far downstream from who we used to be. I tried to write about everyone from the point of view I had during this ridiculous adventure. I was angrier, sadder, and considerably more lost than I am now. If you're in this story, or if I left you out, I hope your present self forgives my past judgments. (Except for that one guy, of course. Fuck that guy.)

The me that lived through this doesn't exist anymore either. I hope that's a good thing.

My dad died before I started writing this book, though you can still find the news about his case in back issues of the *New York Times*. I left my brothers out, not because their stories aren't relevant, but because they have their own stories about this time. They remember things differently, and that's how it should be because their experiences were different than mine. I was talking to one of my brothers about a detail in early on and he said, "Oh no, that couldn't have been the feds. It would have been custody papers. There was a custody thing too." I didn't know at the time, so I didn't write it that way. I didn't go back and change it. I don't want to change what I thought the story was at the time.

Memory is so strange. There are things I remember as though they happened yesterday and other things I can't get at, no matter how I try. I have done what I can with the brain I have.

Writing a book is a crazy undertaking. You sit at the keyboard by yourself, typing and crying—or I did, at least—and it can feel like the loneliest thing you'll ever do. But next to those hard days were some very good ones, in the company of such fine friends. For them, I am truly grateful.

Alex Roberstson Textor insisted I write something for his magazine, *Fields & Stations*, and would not take no for an answer. If he had let me off the hook, this book would not exist. The story I wrote for him tapped a deep vein of words that would not stop flowing until my first draft was done.

A handful of early readers—Suzanne Reismann, Amber Watt, Doug Mack, and Eileen Smith—gave me useful feedback and the confidence to pursue publication. Doug and Eileen were invaluable support in other ways, too, and so generous with their knowledge and experience.

My editor, Jon Arlan, asked hard questions and made me dig deeper into the story; this is a better book for his kind and thoughtful oversight.

I have been so lucky to have my words wrangled by patient and tenacious editors over the course of my writing career and with that in mind, I want thank Sari Botton at *Longreads* for publishing an early version of my "Second Passport" chapter as an excerpt. I am grateful to my writer tribe from the inimitable *World Hum*, especially Jim

Benning, Mike Yessis, and Eva Holland. I am a better writer for your red ink, all of you.

Some time back I connected with Andrew Evans on Twitter and he has been my steadfast companion. While writing this book I joked that he was my Sherpa, helping me carry the heavy things while I crossed the pass—but it's true. Thank you for making the journey easier.

Finally, a note to whoever needs to hear this: I know why you are silent. I know why you stayed. It is never too late to tell your story. You deserve so much better.

I believe you.